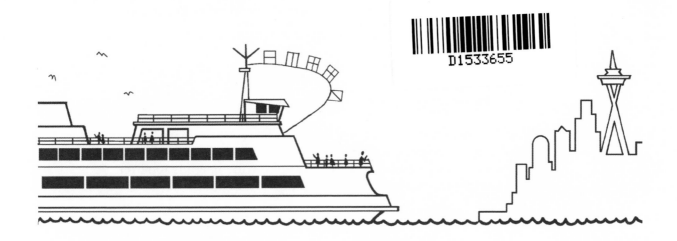

ACROSS THE SOUND

A Guide to Interesting Places West of Puget Sound

Ron Konzak and Mickey Molnaire

[signatures]

To Aunt Sue
+ All the Brooks -
Merry Christmas
2004!

Wind Harp Press
Rolling Bay, Washington

Across The Sound: A Guide to Interesting Places West of Puget Sound

Published by:

Wind Harp Press
PO Box 4494
Rolling Bay, Washington 98061
Tel: (206) 842-4916
www.windharppress.com
Email: feedback@windharppress.com

Wind Harp Press is a division of Konzak Molnaire International, Ltd.

ISBN: 0-9744632-0-5

10 9 8 7 6 5 4 3 2 1

The Publisher and Authors have made every effort to provide accurate,
current information. However, they accept no responsibility for loss,
injury, or inconvenience sustained by any person using this book.

The authors and publisher value your comments and feedback about the
places and businesses mentioned in this guide book. Please send us an
email or drop us a line!

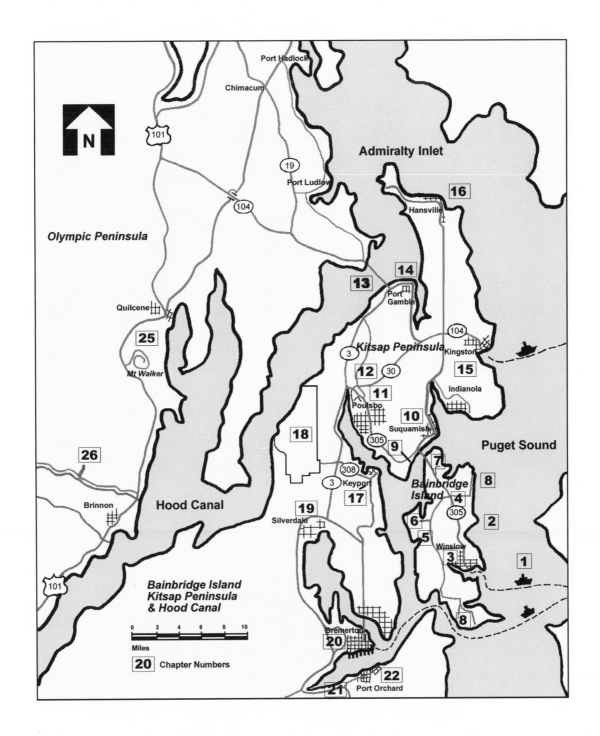

Port Hadlock

Chimacum

101

19

Port Ludlow

104

Admiralty Inlet

16

Hansville

Olympic Peninsula

Quilcene

25

Mt Walker

13

14

Port Gamble

104

Kingston

Kitsap Peninsula

3

12

30

15

Indianola

11

Poulsbo

10

Suquamish

305

9

Puget Sound

18

26

308

7

Brinnon

3 Keyport

17

8

Bainbridge Island

4

305

2

Hood Canal

19

Silverdale

6

5

Winslow

3

1

101

8

Bainbridge Island
Kitsap Peninsula
& Hood Canal

0 2 4 6 8 10

Miles

20 Chapter Numbers

20

Bremerton

21

22

Port Orchard

iii

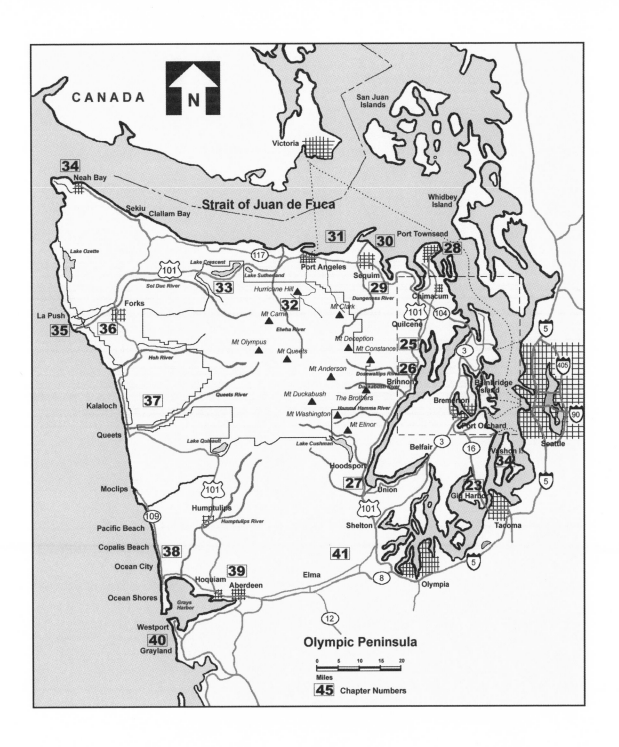

CANADA

N

San Juan
Islands

Victoria

Whidbey
Island

34 Neah Bay

Sekiu
Clallam Bay

Strait of Juan de Fuca

31

30 Port Townsend

28

Lake Ozette

117

Port Angeles

Sequim

Chimacum

Lake Crescent

101

Lake Sutherland

Hurricane Hill

29

Dungeness River

33

Sol Duc River

32

Mt Clark

101

104

Quilcene

Forks

36

Mt Carrie

Elwha River

Mt Deception

25

La Push

35

Mt Olympus

Mt Queets

Mt Constance

3

Bainbridge
Island

Hoh River

Mt Anderson

26

Dosewallips River

Brinnon

Duckabush River

Bremerton

37

Queets River

Mt Duckabush

The Brothers

Hamma Hamma River

Kalaloch

Lake Quinault

Mt Washington

Mt Elinor

Port Orchard

90

Queets

Lake Cushman

Belfair

3

Seattle

Moclips

101

Hoodsport

27

Union

16

Vashon Il.

34

5

109

Humptulips

23

Gig Harbor

Pacific Beach

Humptulips River

Shelton

Tacoma

Copalis Beach

38

41

Ocean City

39

Elma

Ocean Shores

Hoquiam

Aberdeen

8

Olympia

Grays
Harbor

5

Westport

40

Grayland

Olympic Peninsula

12

0   5   10   15   20

Miles

45 Chapter Numbers

CHART OF DISTANCES

Mileage and times are approximate depending on route, traffic, weather and driving style

Chapter	Destination	Bainbridge Ferry Dock		Bremerton Ferry Dock		Kingston Ferry Dock	
		Miles	Hr:Mn	Miles	Hr:Mn	Miles	Hr:Mn
3	Winslow	0	0	30	0:40	21	0:30
4	Bainbridge Winery	0.5	0:03	30	0:45	21	0:30
5	Bainbridge Gardens	3.5	0:07	27	0:45	13.5	0:25
6	Battle Point Park	5.5	0:09	25	0:48	16	0:26
7	Bloedel Reserve	6.8	0:10	24	0:45	10	0:15
8	Fay-Bainbridge State Park	6.5	:10	26	0:48	18	0:25
8	Fort Ward State Park	7	0:13	37	0:58	28	0:41
9	Suquamish Tribal Center & Museum	8.8	0:12	22	0:30	14	0:21
10	Suquamish	8.5	0:14	24	0:32	7.5	0:10
11	Poulsbo	13	0:19	19	0:21	8.5	0:12
12	Central Market	14	0:20	19	0:21	8.5	0:12
13	Hood Canal Bridge	20	0:30	23	0:30	8	0:12
14	Port Gamble	21	0:31	24	0:36	8	0:12
15	Indianola & Kingston	21	0:31	24	0:36	0	0
16	Point No Point	26	0:40	40	1:00	8.8	0:14
17	Keyport	20	0:30	16	0:17	16	0:20
18	Sub Base Bangor	18	0:25	12	0:16	16	0:20
19	Silverdale	20	0:30	9	0:12	16	0:20
20	Bremerton	30	0:40	0	0	26	0:45
21	Elandan Gardens	34	0:45	4	0:15	30	0:45
22	Port Orchard	41	0:55	11	0:20	37	0:50
23	Vashon Island-Southworth Ferry Dock	51	0:56	21	0:39	49	1:05
24	Gig Harbor	73	1:40	43	1:05	69	1:35

CHART OF DISTANCES CONTINUED

Chapter	Destination	Bainbridge Ferry Dock		Bremerton Ferry Dock		Kingston Ferry Dock	
		Miles	Hr:Mn	Miles	Hr:Mn	Miles	Hr:Mn
25	Mount Walker	40	1:00	43	1:05	34	0:50
26	Rocky Brook Falls	60	1:30	63	1:05	48	1:00
26	Brinnon	57	1:28	60	1:35	45	0:55
27	Lake Cushman & South Hood Canal	61	1:15	31	0:40	34	0:51
28	Port Townsend	46	1:00	49	1:05	34	0:51
29	Sequim	53	1:08	60	1:10	45	0:55
30	Dungeness Spit	53	1:08	60	1:10	45	0:55
31	Port Angeles	70	1:30	73	1:30	58	1:10
32	Hurricane Ridge	87	2:00	90	2:00	75	1:40
33	Lake Crescent	93	1:55	96	2:00	81	1:50
33	Sol Duck Hot Springs	114	2:35	119	2:40	104	2:30
34	Neah Bay	142	3:15	148	3:20	133	3:05
35	La Push	135	2:40	138	2:45	123	2:30
36	Forks	135	2:40	138	2:45	123	2:30
37	Hoh Rain Forest	158	3:40	168	3:45	153	3:30
37	Kalaloch	162	3:05	165	3:10	150	2:55
37	Lake Quinault	194	3:40	197	3:45	182	3:30
38	Moclips	210	4:05	213	4:10	198	4:55
38	Ocean Shores	230	4:35	233	4:40	218	4:25
39	Aberdeen & Hoquiam	242	4:50	245	4:55	230	4:40
40	Westport	266	5:25	269	5:30	254	5:15
41	Elma & Shelton	287	5:55	290	6:00	275	5:35

To our many guests over the years who inspired this book and help to keep us continuously aware of the beautiful, magical place in which we live.

Ron Konzak and Mickey Molnaire
Fuurin-Oka Futon & Breakfast

About the Authors

Ron Konzak and Mickey Molnaire own and operate Fuurin-Oka Futon and Breakfast, a traditional Japanese guest house and garden on Bainbridge Island, Washington.

Across the Sound is Ron's third book. His first was a self-help workbook, *Lifegraph* (Metamorphous Press, 1985), which he followed with a whimsical cookbook for Ramen noodles, *The Book of Ramen* (Turtleback Books, 1993). Both he and Mickey love to cook, and Mickey is currently working on two cookbooks of her own.

Ron moved to Bainbridge in 1965. He was a member of the Mountaineers for many years. Mickey came to the area in 1979, and did a brief stint on the National Ski Patrol before she met Ron and moved to the island.

One of the reasons Ron and Mickey became innkeepers is because they themselves enjoy travelling, meeting people and learning about other cultures and languages. Ron has travelled through Europe as musical director of a dance troupe, journeyed through Japan with Buddhist monks, and lived in a rural Korean village.

Mickey taught English overseas for many years, living in Germany, Switzerland, and Iran. They were married in Edinburgh, travelled together in Scotland, England and Ireland, and have at least a working knowledge of about 10 languages between them.

Hosting a bed and breakfast gives them the opportunity to share their many interests with guests from all over the world. Ron is an architect, musician, woodworker and harp maker. He played in the 70s soft rock trio Pierymplezak and the Irish trio Pratai. But Ron had always wanted to design and build an authentic traditional Japanese house, and Fuurin-Oka is a fulfillment of that life-long ambition.

Mickey is also a musician, and she performs with Ron as Foggynotions. The two were also members of the Celtic fusion band The Islanders Five. In addition, Mickey is a computer consultant specializing in training and support for small businesses and non-profit organizations.

CONTENTS

ACKNOWLEDGEMENTS

We had a wonderful time driving around and meeting so many friendly and helpful people in chambers of commerce, visitors centers, museums, bed and breakfasts, restaurants, shops, etc., who loved to tell us stories about the places they live. Without them, this book would not exist.

We would like to thank the Bentryn family of Bainbirdge Vineyards and Winery, Chris and Junkoh Harui of Bainbridge Gardens, Richard Brown of the Bloedel Reserve, and Larry Nakata of Town & Country Markets for their time and help.

Special thanks go to Corby Ingold, Meg Hagemann, Bob Spafford and Wini Jones, who proofread the manuscript, Bob Burback who lent us that huge book on the history of Kitsap County, Terry Domico who encouraged us to become publishers, and our many guests who field-tested the chapters and gave us their valuable feedback.

INTRODUCTION

Seattle and Puget Sound attract many visitors every year. We are proud to be living in a place that has so much to offer, and we love to point out its finest attractions.

However, many visitors reach the eastern shore of Puget Sound and stop. While the Space Needle, Pike Place Market and the Seattle waterfront are memorable visits, we here on the peninsulas feel that people are missing out on the best that this area has to offer — and it's only a pleasant ferry trip away.

We own and operate a bed and breakfast on Bainbridge Island and have a constant stream of visitors throughout the year. The question most asked is: "Do you have any suggestions for interesting places to see?"

You bet we do. They are places we visit ourselves, not only because they are nearby but because they are so exceptional. We often say that if we lived somewhere else, we would be coming here for vacation.

In describing these places to guests, we found we were constantly repeating ourselves, so we started typing out a list of nearby attractions and destinations to give them.

Then we expanded the list to a page of information about each attraction. We started with places close to Bainbridge Island and Seattle, but gradually began to extend our scope to include the entire Kitsap and Olympic Peninsulas. It wasn't long before we realized that we had an entire book in the making.

Experimenting on our guests, we learned what visitors wanted to know about our area. So we included information on lodging, restaurants, weather, as well as stories, background and history.

Ron once drove a tour van for a local tour operator and was able to design his own tour. He called it "Places Where Tourists Don't Usually Go". In this book we have included the places that are often overlooked as visitors head for the spots on the official Washington State visitor brochures.

The fact is, we have an abundance of interesting and scenic places that really deserve to be visited — some for their breathtaking natural beauty and some for their colorful local history.

We hope this little book inspires you to discover new and exciting places and embark upon your own adventures.

Ron Konzak & Mickey Molnaire

When you visit the land across the sound from Seattle, you will probably come by way of one of the Washington State Ferries. There are four ferry routes from the greater Seattle area: from the Fauntleroy terminal in southwest Seattle to Vashon Island and south Kitsap (50 minutes); from Coleman Dock in downtown Seattle to Bainbridge Island (35 minutes) or Bremerton (60 minutes); and from Edmonds, north of Seattle, to Kingston in north Kitsap County (30 minutes). Additional ferries make up a total of ten routes throughout the Sound. In one year the system carries 11 million cars and 27 million people. The state operates the ferry system as a part of its highway department.

Somewhere between 40 and 50 percent of the adult population of Bainbridge Island works in the greater Seattle area. If you happen to be on a peak hour commuter boat, you will witness a bit of cross-sound life: people reading, eating, sleeping, playing cards, talking on cell phones, working on laptops, walking laps around the deck. On the morning runs, the restrooms are full of men shaving or changing from their motorcycle gear and women putting on make-up and plying hair dryers and curling irons for last-minute coiffures.

Commuters ride the ferries so often that they sometimes come to believe that they have customary and therefore reserved seats. In reality there is no such thing, but if you start to sit down and receive a cold glare, you will realize that you have crossed an invisible line. How you handle it is up to you.

On less hectic runs you are liable to hear an itinerant musician playing a harp, violin, cello or dulcimer, and at Christmas time you may find a group of carolers in Victorian attire.

Occasionally you may also be entertained by passing through flotillas of pleasure boats or salmon fishermen, or pods of Orca whales (also fishing for salmon). Dramatic sunrises and sunsets and stunning views of Mount Rainier and Mount Baker are also possible, weather permitting.

In fact, ferry travel can be very entertaining and refreshing if one does not allow oneself to become jaded by a daily commute. At the same time it is somewhat daunting to consider the possibility that, according to Washington State Ferries, over the course of a 40-year career a ferry commuter will have spent more than a year on the boat and will have logged enough miles to have circumnavigated the earth SIX times.

The most frustrating part of ferry travel is the waiting, especially if you are driving a car on. (In our local vernacular we refer to bringing a car on board as "driving on", as in "Did you walk on or drive on?") The worst possible situation is to forget that you drove on, and simply walk off the ferry with your car still on board. This has happened to more islanders than would care to admit it.

Because of the ferry's popularity with visitors and importance to local transportation, a ferry can fill up quickly and leave you waiting for the next one. **The rule of thumb is to be at the ferry dock one boat ahead of the one you want to catch.** On holidays, Friday evenings westbound and Sunday evenings eastbound, you might want to make that *two* boats ahead.

Islanders and West Sounders are fairly philosophical about missing the ferry they were aiming for, so take a tip from them if you find yourself with some time to spend before the next boat. Fret not, get a gate pass (so you can get back to your car without paying again) and take a walk north along the waterfront. Get some fish and chips and feed the seagulls at Ivar's. Or stroll into some of the gift shops that line the shore. You might make it to the waterfront park at the Aquarium, but don't try to do the Pike Place Market—you will be pushing your luck—save that for a special visit..

Be sure to get back to your car 15-20 minutes before the ferry is scheduled to depart, or you may find yourself waiting for *another* boat. Ferries generally start loading 10-15 minutes before the departure time. Walk-on (or run-on) passengers have a little more lee-way.

There are a few rules and regulations you need to be aware of:

1. On many runs including Bainbridge, car fares are charged in both directions, but passenger fares are charged in only one direction (westbound).

2. It is a courtesy to turn off your headlights and use only parking lights (or none) in the ferry ticket booth and parking areas, on-loading as well as off-loading. After dark they are amply lit, and you will only unnecessarily hamper the vision of the ferry workers.

3. Hazardous materials are not allowed on board, and that includes gas cans. RVs need to shut down their propane systems.

4. Once the boat is moving, all engines must be turned off. No matter how cold it is. Go upstairs and get a latte. And don't restart your engine until you get the signal from the deckhand—or everyone around you does.

5. Smoking is restricted to designated areas, usually on the top deck of the boat. *Never* on the car deck. Smoking during loading and unloading is not allowed.

6. ***Please*** do not set your car alarm!!! — unless you want to be embarrassed. Normal motion of the vessel is likely to set it off, and the captain will announce the model of your car and your license number over the PA system.

Information
Washington State Ferries, 206/464-6400, 888/808-7977 (WA & B.C.)800/84-FERRY (WA & B.C.) *wsdot.wa.gov/ferries*

2 BAINBRIDGE ISLAND

Frog Rock

We're going to start with Bainbridge Island because it is the center of *our* world: we live here. Bainbridge is also usually the first place that visitors come to when they venture across the Sound, because the Washington State Ferry system is the most popular attraction in Western Washington, and the most popular run is from downtown Seattle to Bainbridge.

The island, about the size of Manhattan, was part of the collection of communities on Puget Sound once served by the "Mosquito Fleet" of small, private steamships. It became the natural gateway to the Kitsap and Olympic Peninsulas in 1950 when the bridge at Agate Passage was built at the north end.

However, many people drive off the ferry up the highway and over the bridge in a hurry to get somewhere else, and may not take the time to see what interesting things the island has to offer. We will cover many of the individual attractions in detail in the next few chapters.

Bainbridge Island before Europeans was a centuries-old summer food-gathering area for the Suquamish tribe. There are still petroglyphs to be seen at the northern tip of the island. Check with the Historical Museum for directions.

Puget Sound was explored by the British and Americans from 1792 onward. They discovered some of the best deep water harbors in the whole area on Bainbridge: Eagle Harbor and Port Madison Bay, followed closely by Port Blakely Harbor. Port Madison and Port Blakely became the locations for rival sawmills, and at one time the mill at Port Blakely was the largest in the world. President Rutherford B. Hayes visited Port Blakely in 1891, and didn't bother to go over to Seattle! A waterfront park is now being developed where the mill once stood.

Near Port Blakely today is the new **IslandWood** environmental learning center, with the focus of providing environmental education for disadvantaged youth in a camp-like setting. The creation of this ecofriendly and imaginative project has been the passion of software giant Paul Brainerd and his wife Debbi. Additional courses and lectures are open to the general public throughout the year.

There are two beachfront state parks on Bainbridge, the world-famous **Bloedel Reserve** gardens, and 18 developed and undeveloped parks and facilities operated by the local park district, including a recently completed state-of-the-art skate board park at **Strawberry Hill Park.**

The waters offshore hold wonders for divers, whether it is playing with octopi at Octopus Rock in Rich Passage, or riding the tidal currents under the Agate "Pass" (as it is locally called) Bridge.

Artists, musicians and writers are well represented among the local population. Bainbridge is also known for the high number of enthusiastic gardeners among its residents. (A few years ago we were searching mail-order companies all over the US and Canada for certain rose varieties—and they *all* knew Bainbridge Island.) Five or six of our private gardens are featured annually during the **Bainbridge in Bloom Garden Tour** in early July, a fundraiser for the local arts council.

The annual **Rotary Club Rummage Sale and Auction**, which raises money for many charitable organizations in the community, is one of the largest events of its kind anywhere. Thrill to the spectacle of thousands of people running for sailboats, cars, lawnmowers, skis, furniture, building supplies, bicycles, books, blenders, etc., at the moment the barriers are dropped. This extravaganza usually takes place on the weekend before the Fourth of July.

Another annual event in February brings 4,000 plus bicyclists to the island for **Chilly Hilly**, a 33-mile loop ride on backroads that is considered one of the top classic rides in the nation. The ride is truly "hilly", with an overall elevation gain of 2,500 feet, but even so, many cyclists ride the route during the rest of the year.

Along the Chilly Hilly route in the northeast quadrant of the Island you will certainly come upon a local landmark and icon, **Frog Rock**.

This giant boulder at the intersection of North Madison and Phelps Road, was dynamited by the county some years ago after a car crashed into it. The county's efforts were not very successful, breaking off two large chunks: what is now the frog's head, and the ladybug companion rock, but otherwise hardly damaging the main rock.

Later, county workers placed the head rock back on top of the base, and a creative local artist saw a green frog with red lips in the whole thing. Frog Rock was an important guidepost in the days before the island roads all had names, and remains a treasured oddity today.

Bainbridge Island has recently gained attention as the real-life location of *Snow Falling on Cedars*, by local author David Guterson. This best-selling suspense novel (and beautiful motion picture) tells the story of the internment of all citizens and residents of Japanese ancestry living on the West Coast at the outbreak of World War II. Bainbridge was the place where the first group of Japanese-Americans was forcibly evacuated.

Two characters in the book were based on real people: Walt and Millie Woodward, editors of the island newspaper. Risking loss of popularity and advertisers, and even incurring death threats, the Woodwards continued to question the breach of the US Constitution that put their friends and neighbors in internment camps. They published article after article throughout the war criticizing the government's policy. They also hired some of the islanders in the camps as correspondents to provide news back to their neighbors on the island.

Today the Bainbridge Island Japanese-American community together with many other residents are working to make the location of the old ferry dock at the foot of Taylor Avenue a National Historic Monument. The full story of those times, as well as many other aspects of island history, can be learned at the **Bainbridge Island Historical Museum**, which was just recently relocated a short distance from the ferry in downtown Winslow.

Information
Bainbridge Island Park & Recreation District, 206/842-2306, *biparks.org*
Bainbridge Island Historical Society & Museum, 215 Ericksen Av, 206/842-2773, *bicomnet.com/bihs*
IslandWood, 206/855-4333, *islandwood.org*
Bainbridge In Bloom Garden Tour, 206/842-7901, *artshum.org*
Chilly HillyBike Ride, Cascade Bicycle Club *Cascade.org/chilly_hilly*

WINSLOW

City Hall, Bainbridge Island

Winslow pulses to the rhythm of the ferry schedule. Every 45 minutes or so, a Washington State ferry disgorges hundreds of cars and thousands of passengers. After a flurry of activity and traffic, the commuters and visitors are absorbed into the island and beyond, and once again, tranquility reigns — at least until the next ferry docks, when it starts all over again.

Having ferry traffic through their town is a distinction that some islanders could do without, but despite the grumbling, many islanders enjoy the proximity to Seattle, happily taking the ferry to a Mariners or Seahawks game, glad to leave their cars behind. And daily some 8,000 commuting foot passengers take the ferry. If you happen to take the ferry at the same times that they do, you'll have an opportunity to meet many of them yourself.

Winslow was formerly known as the City of Winslow, once the only incorporated part of the island and the largest town. But in 1991 in a fairly unprecedented move, it annexed the rest of the island and changed its name to the City of Bainbridge Island. Since incorporation,

Bainbridge has grown in sophistication, building a new city hall and surfacing its own roads. The downtown area is still known as Winslow and is the cultural and commercial capital of the island.

Visitors will find a town full of interesting shops, art galleries, restaurants and people all within a short walk of the ferry terminal. There is an information kiosk at the ferry terminal and a visitors' center at the Chamber of Commerce that will deluge you with information. A pleasant walk leads from the ferry terminal along the waterfront, past the shipyard where the state maintains the ferries, into **Waterfront Park**, where many events take place at the boat-shaped bandstand, including summer evening concerts. You can rent a variety of boats to explore Eagle Harbor and cruise among its colorful live-aboard community, featuring some interesting water craft.

Bainbridge Performing Arts, a community theater group active since 1956, operates a theater featuring local theater productions, improv comedy and other special events. Check their website for upcoming events.

Visit the unique **Haiku Garden** at the public library, a gift to the island from the Bainbridge Japanese-American community. The library also features public art by several island artists and surrounding gardens planted and maintained by volunteers.

Gardeners will also enjoy the island's two main nurseries: **Bainbridge Gardens**, with a history warranting its own chapter (see page 11), and **Bay Hay and Feed**, with the bonus attraction of baby chicks and ducklings in the spring.

On the subject of gardens, the **Little and Lewis Garden Gallery** features unique garden art: nature-based sculptures, mirrors and paintings in concrete. Their work has had international acclaim and has been featured in books, magazines, and on TV. Oversized pomegranates on Tuscan columns, giant Gunnera leaves, paintings resembling fragments of ancient frescoes are among the designs that can be seen in their garden gallery in Winslow. Many involve water features. George Little and David Lewis have transformed their small suburban lot into a lush tropical paradise. Call for an appointment.

Another specialty garden stop is **MesoGeo Greenhouse**. Terri Stanley, a landscape architect who has been captivated by plants of Mediterranean origin or inclination, has created a greenhouse and nursery full of rare finds which has become a magnet for collectors.

Sometime in May at the height of the Scotch broom blooming season, people decorate themselves and their kids and bikes and dogs with fronds of Scotch broom, a noxious weed with no natural enemies in its adopted land. It has overtaken the island as well as much of Western Washington annually gracing the landscape with beautiful golden blossoms, followed by oily, half-dead looking foliage and vigorous seed pods. A parade and tiddly-winks tournament, all tongue-in-cheek, uses enough of the stuff to symbolically get rid of it. The **Scotch Broom Festival** is Washington State's most elusive festival. The date is kept secret, and the event is suddenly sprung upon the town of Winslow. If you happen to be there, you see it -- if not, you don't. The newest member of the Kiwanis Club may be privy to the inside information.

The **Grand Old Fourth** typifies the close-knit small-town community and love of fun and parties that seem to peak out during the summer. A week-long schedule of events, including an evening street dance, culminates with a huge community pancake breakfast, street fair and the main event -- a parade with Dixieland band, bagpipes, clowns, kids on decorated bikes and politicians waving from convertibles. With most of the island in the parade, it's a good thing that the celebration attracts a number of folks from Seattle and other localities, otherwise there would scarcely be anyone to watch and cheer.

Directions: From the ferry, turn left at the first traffic signal.

Information:
Bainbridge Island Chamber of Commerce, 206/842-3700, *bainbridgechamber.com*
Bainbridge Island City Hall, 206/842-7633, *ci.bainbridge-isl.wa.us*
Bainbridge Arts and Crafts, 151 Winslow Way East, 206/842-3132, *bainbridgeartsandcrafts.org*
Bainbridge Performing Arts 206/842-8569, *bpa-playhouse.org*
Bainbridge Island Arts & Humanities Council, 206/842-7901, *artshum.org*
Bay Hay and Feed, 10355 NE Valley Rd, 206/842-2813
Little & Lewis Garden Gallery, 206/842-8327, *littleandlewis.com*. Advance appointment required, April to October. For public garden open days, check the website. For sculpture purchases or commissions, call for an appointment year round.
MesoGeo, 206/780-1331 *mesogeogarden.com*, call for appointment.

4 BAINBRIDGE ISLAND VINEYARDS & WINERY

Bainbridge Island Winery

When you drive off the ferry onto Bainbridge Island, you may be speeding up the highway and over the bridge before you realize that you have passed the **Bainbridge Island Vineyards & Winery**, one of the most unique wineries in the Puget Sound area. The winery has moved from the old location near the Winslow ferry to a new spot amid the vineyards on Day Road East about 5 miles north on Highway 305.

Following the European tradition of fine wine makers, it is entirely family-owned and operated by the Bentryns, who live on the premises, grow all the grapes, and make and bottle the wine there. Their wine is only sold in a little shop in the corner of their big barn and in some local restaurants and markets. If you stop for a visit, they will offer you a taste of their award-winning wines.

The Bentryns settled in this particular area because the climate so closely approximated that of the great wine growing areas of France and Germany. The grapes that they grow are descendants of the grapes that are native to those areas and already have a great international reputation.

They have recently added to their repertoire of traditional grape wines some fine fruit wines from the almost legendary island-grown strawberries and raspberries.

Gerard Bentryn learned wine-making from famous vintners in Europe by working with them in the vineyards, tending the vines as well as harvesting and helping them make the wine. His enthusiasm for his work is shared by his whole family, who make your visit a fun and interesting experience. The family cheerfully admits that they wouldn't be doing all this work if it weren't a lot of fun. They have even hosted several Oktoberfest celebrations in the past, replete with oompah bands, yodeling, polka dancing, and, of course, lots of wine and beer.

The Bentryns also contributed considerable energy to getting western Washington wineries on the map through the establishment of the Puget Sound Appelation.

Gerard is justifiably proud of being one of a small but dedicated group of people on the island who own and operate farms. They get together every Saturday morning to offer their wares at a regular **Farmers Market** in the parking lot of the City Hall in Winslow. Here you will have an opportunity to buy a variety of fruits, vegetables, preserves and baked goods, home-made soaps and crafts. Local musicians also add to the festivities.

Bainbridge Island Winery, 8989 Day Road East, ½ mile east of Hwy 305, 206/ 842-WINE (842-9463) *bainbridgevineyards.com*. Please call for hours & directions.

Bainbridge Island Farmer's Market, 10 AM to 1 PM Saturdays, May through September, 206/780-9445, bainbridgefarmersmarket.com

BAINBRIDGE GARDENS

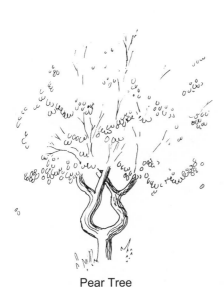

Pear Tree

Bainbridge Gardens was a thriving and popular destination garden and nursery as far back as 1920. Zenhichi Harui, who came to this country from Japan as a young man in 1910, planted trees and moved earth and formed ponds and streams to create a beautiful environment for people to enjoy. It became a favorite destination for visitors to the island, in a similar manner to Butchart Gardens in Victoria, B.C., including a sunken garden with colorful carp, overhanging willows and sculptured lions' heads.

Then, at the height of its popularity, the second world war broke out, and the family relocated in eastern Washington for the duration. Upon their return at the war's end, they found the gardens in total disrepair: greenhouses broken, blackberries covering everything and nursery stock hopelessly overgrown. The gardens never recovered during Zenhichi's lifetime, but in 1990 his son Junkoh decided to take on the challenge of restoring the gardens and nursery.

The red pine trees that his father loved have become a special place, a grove to walk through and enjoy. Trees that his father painstakingly trained now form a memorial garden, including a pear tree he had grafted and shaped in such a way that the trunk split, turned outward, and then rejoined to form the outline of a pear.

Now Bainbridge Gardens is again a destination for visitors who enjoy all the things that gardeners love. In the midst of all the nursery plants and garden statuary is the New Rose Cafe, a pleasant place to refresh yourself. In true Northwest tradition, you can get an espresso along with a light lunch including pizza or homemade pastries from the ovens, and afterwards take a stroll on one of the nature trails.

Call or check the web site for information on the frequent garden lectures and workshops, many featuring nationally-known garden writer and islander Ann Lovejoy. There is no charge to visit the nursery and grounds; some lectures and workshops may require a small fee.

Bainbridge Gardens is located at 9415 Miller Road, 3 miles south of the intersection of Highway 305 and Day Road, or 2 miles north of the intersection of High School Road and Miller Road. *Winter Hours:* Mondays through Saturdays 9:00 A.M. to 5:30 P.M., Sundays 10 A.M. to 4:00 P.M. Summer hours slightly longer. 206/842-5888, *bainbridgegardens.com*

BATTLE POINT PARK
AND RITCHIE OBSERVATORY

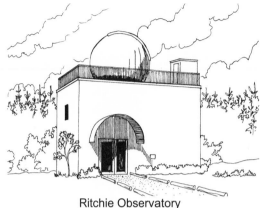

Ritchie Observatory

This popular 83-acre public park is named for a historical point, just west of the park, where a battle took place around 1860 -- not between the settlers and the Indians, but between the local Suquamish tribe and the Haida from the north.

The Haida often raided other tribes and took slaves. They had planned a surprise attack on the Suquamish who were camping at the point. But the Suquamish were alerted by a cannon shot from the trading post on Agate Passage, across from the present town of Suquamish, which signaled a warning and allowed them to ambush the attackers and turn back the invasion.

The location of the park itself is also considered historical because it was the partner site of the giant receiving antenna and code school at Fort Ward, at the south end of the island, which helped break the Japanese military code during the Second World War, an important step in deciding the outcome of that war. The transmitter at Battle Point then relayed the information to Washington, D.C. Some of the original buildings are still standing. After the war, the base became

surplus property and was donated to the community.

The U.S. Army then took it on as an engineering exercise, moving earth around and forming the picturesque ponds and hills to the north and the athletic fields to the south. Groves of trees now harbor picnic facilities, and a walking and a jogging trail circles the perimeter.

Also available to the public are "pea patch" garden plots and tennis courts, playgrounds, and the whole park is ringed by bridle trails. Once a year, in early June, the park hosts the **Bainbridge Classic**, a regional show jumping competition which attracts many horse enthusiasts.

Kids Up Playground. The newest addition to the park is an incredibly imaginative playground complex, built by local volunteers in the summer of 2001. Additional elements continue to appear. Young and old will appreciate the playful spirit of this endeavor.

Just outside the north entrance to the park on the other side of Frey Road is the trail to **Fairy Dell Park**, as magical as its name suggests. The path winds ¼ mile along a stream through some of the largest old-growth trees on the island. The trail also provides access to the beach between Arrow Point and Battle Point. A walking stick will come in handy for maneuvering some spots.

Ritchie Observatory at the center of the park is a stout, block-like building, next to which originally stood the giant antenna, transmitting decoded signals from points across the Pacific. The building housed the power unit which served the transmitter.

This reinforced-concrete building is now the base of the Ritchie Observatory and telescope.

Ed Ritchie, a local resident and inventor, designed and built the giant telescope and the supporting electronic equipment. John Rudolph, a local architect, not only adapted the building to its new function, but built the dome which houses the new telescope. John was right at home having been also instrumental in the original design of the park. Ed and John were supported by a dedicated group of islanders who formed the Bainbridge Island Astronomical Association.

The giant 27.5" reflecting mirror, a government surplus item from the "Star Wars" project, was donated to the group by Boeing, and is the heart of this amazing state-of-the-art telescope, one of the largest amateur telescopes on the West Coast.

Of all of Ed Ritchie's many inventions and accomplishments, the telescope was his masterpiece. He designed and built the mechanism to grind and polish the mirror to its finished curvature, built the telescope housing, designed the computerized tracking system, and also built the machine that electronically magnified the image so that it could be viewed on a screen by a small audience. He died in 1997, just before the completion of his work, but left complete drawings and instructions that enabled the group to carry on and complete the

project. The observatory was officially opened in 1999 and dedicated to him.

John Rudolph will be remembered for having devised a way to "remodel" the massive concrete element in the middle of the building and to raise money for the Association at the same time by raffling off the right to hit the TNT plunger.

Visitors to the observatory can take a tour conducted by BAA volunteers every other Saturday afternoon. Although clouds obscure the view many days of the year, our frequent rains wash the sky of impurities making for crystal-clear viewing opportunities on clear nights. Star parties are held at least once a month -- call or check the web site for dates.

Directions: From Winslow take Highway 305 north to High School Road. Turn left (west) on and follow High School Road to its end at the T-junction with Miller Road. Turn right (north) and continue to Arrow Point Drive. Turn left (west) and continue to the entrance of the park. Turn left inside the park and follow the road to the observatory.

Directions:
From Winslow/the ferry terminal drive north on 305 to High School Road. Turn left and go until the road ends in a "T" at Fletcher Bay Rd. Turn right and go north to Arrow Point Drive. Turn left and follow the road to the park.

Information:
Battle Point Park -- Bainbridge Island Parks & Recreation 206/842-2306, *biparks.org*
Hours: Dawn till dusk, except for the night star parties
Ritchie Observatory -- Battle Point Astronomical Association 206/842-9152
bicomnet.com/ritchieobs/
Star parties held once a month on the Saturday closest to the first quarter of the moon, starting at dusk. Tours are given during the day on the second and fourth Saturdays.
Bainbridge Classic 206/842-7776

THE BLOEDEL RESERVE

Visitor Center, Bloedel Reserve

The **Bloedel Reserve** was specially created to be fully enjoyed without interpretation or explanation. It is definitely not a conventional arboretum or botanical garden, but a wonderful concept with naught but the sheer delight of the soul as its mission.

Unexpected floral bursts blend sensitively along a forest path, swans reflect in a forest pond, flowers whimsically appear amidst native greenery. A mind-boggling variety of ground-covers blend the cultivated areas into the natural landscape.

This was Prentice Bloedel's vision: to create a place where one can come for an hour or an afternoon and walk in the woods; a retreat where one can escape life's daily pressures. There is an illusion of being alone, a sense of privacy. You can follow the trails that lead from vista to vista, through woodlands, along ponds and to fasci-nating places like the dramatic 200-foot-long Reflection Pool surrounded by a yew hedge, or

the cool green dampness of the moss garden, or the thoughtfully-placed stones of the Japanese Zen garden.

At the center of approximately 150 acres of this natural and man-made sanctuary, on a bluff surrounded by formal trees and shrubs, sits a classically-proportioned French country mansion which now serves as a visitors' center. This was the residence of Prentice and Virginia Bloedel for thirty years and is now a center for receptions, gardening lectures, and concerts by talented local artists. The Reserve is administered by the Arbor Fund, which offers a membership to the Bloedel Reserve, the benefits of which are unlimited visits and advance reservations to all its activities and programs.

The Reserve began its modern history in 1856, when 67 acres were dedicated by President James Buchanan to benefit the establishment of a territorial university. The land was logged and the proceeds contributed to the first campus of the University of Washington, located in downtown Seattle.

In 1904, Mrs. John Collins, wife of the mayor of Seattle, bought the land for a weekend and summer beach retreat. J. Lister Holmes designed and built the 18th century-style mansion between 1928 and 1931. Mrs. Collins named the estate "Collinswood".

The Bloedels acquired the property in 1953, calling it "Agate Point Farm", and expanding it to 150 acres. They constructed barns for sheep and chickens, planted vegetable gardens, and began the creation of the formal gardens.

In 1955, Fujitaro Kubota (best known for the gardens which bear his name in the Rainier Valley area of Seattle) designed and planted the

Japanese garden, and the Japanese guest house by Paul Hayden Kirk was completed in 1960. Almost any book or magazine article on Japanese gardens in the U.S. will include photos of this garden.

The Bloedels made a gift of the Reserve to the University of Washington in 1970, but later purchased it back in 1986 to preserve their original vision: not a horticultural garden with labels on all the plants, but a personal experience of nature.

The Gatehouse was started in 1986 and the Bloedel Reserve opened to the public in 1988.

The boardwalk through the bog was constructed in 1992, using only tools that could be hand-carried into the sensitive wetland area.

Other highlights of the Reserve are the Bird Refuge, Orchid Trail, Camellia Walk, Waterfall Overlook, Birch Garden and Rhododendron Glen.

Specimen plants to look for are *Parrotia persica* on the Mid Pond, with its fabulous fall color; the Himalayan fir (*Abies spectabilis*) on the lawn together with the Atlas cedar (*Cedrus atlantica*) and the Empress tree (*Paulownia tomentosa*).

The patio features two weeping Camperdown elm trees (*Ulnus glabra var camperdownii*) which were planted by Mrs. Collins; the copper beech (*Fagus purpurea*) on the north side of the house; and the lace cap hydrangeas (*Hydrangea macrophylla*) near the Christmas Pool.

Trumpeter swans and tundra swans inhabit the waterfall area and midpond, and have provided breeding stock for other gardens in North America.

No new formal gardens are planned; rather the future focus is on the contrast between the natural and formal areas. New plantings will emphasize the use of native plants in natural settings and as ornamentals.

Reservations are required, as only 40 people are admitted into the gardens at any given time, ensuring a private and uncrowded experience for all. But unless you are aiming for Mother's Day or high-volume summer weekends, you can usually get in the same day you call.

Also located on the Reserve is the Island Wildlife Shelter, a volunteer non-profit organization that rescues and releases sick, injured, or orphaned wild birds and animals . They also offer advice and education on wildlife to the public.

Directions: You can reach the Bloedel Reserve by taking Agate Loop Road from Highway 305 about one-half mile south of the Agate Pass bridge. Follow the signs to the main gate.

Information:

Bloedel Reserve: 7571 NE Dolphin Dr. Call 206/842-7631 to schedule your visit. *Hours:* Wednesday through Sunday from 10 AM to 4 PM everyday except federal holidays. Admission is $10 per person, $8 for seniors and $6 for children 5-12, children under 5 are free. *bloedelreserve.org*

Island Wildlife Shelter: 7501 NE Dolphin Dr. 206/855-9057

8 FAY-BAINBRIDGE & FORT WARD STATE PARKS

Seattle from Fay-Bainbridge Beach

Fay-Bainbridge State Park

Although Bainbridge Island has 48 miles of shoreline, precious few waterfront areas are available for public access and recreation. The most popular of them is Fay-Bainbridge State Park. It's not named, as you might think, for the charming young daughter of Captain Bainbridge. Instead it combines the name of the donor of the property, Dr. Temple S. Fay (a professor at the University of Washington) with the namesake of the island, the American naval captain who spent most of his career around Algeria and aboard the USS Constitution and never, ever, came to the western side of this continent, let alone Puget Sound.

Located on the island's northeast shore, the park has an unobstructed close-up view of the Sound. The scenery is excellent, with a major volcano at each end—Mount Baker and Mount Rainier—and the city of Seattle somewhere in the middle. You can clamber over the several yards of driftwood and walk along the water. There is usually good

wind for kites. We once watched a lunar eclipse from our seats on a driftwood log.

The historic bell at the entrance, which came from San Francisco in 1883, was originally intended for the school house at Port Madison. It wandered around the island, spending time in various locations, until it was finally placed at the park.

The park has 10 tent and 26 RV overnight campsites, each with a table and fireplace. RV sites have water only and a few of them will accommodate RV's over 30 feet long. All camping is first-come, first-served.

The day-use area includes picnic tables, two covered kitchen shelters, playground equipment, swimming beach and modern restroom facilities with hot showers. There are horseshoe pits, volleyball posts, and a children's play area. Two mooring-buoys and an RV dumping station complete the park's facilities. (In the old days there was a refreshment stand called the "Sand Spit Snack Shack"—say *that* 5 times fast—but it has since passed into oblivion.)

The adjacent Point Monroe sand spit is residential, with rustic summer cottages and palatial homes jammed shoulder to shoulder, tenuously perched, defying the winter storms and tsunamis.

The lagoon formed by the spit is a good place to watch shorebirds. There is a large heron rookery nearby across the road from Kane Cemetery.

Fort Ward State Park

Along an old abandoned access road on the south side of the island is Fort Ward State Park, a hiker's, cyclist's and birder's delight. Named for Brigadier General George H. Ward, it has a rather nonviolent military history. Originally commissioned as a military base in 1900, the current park contains two of four gun batteries that were installed to guard Rich Passage as the last line of defense for the Naval Shipyard in Bremerton. The Vinton battery, along the shore at the south end of the park, had six 3-inch guns. The more interesting uphill Thornburgh battery is a bit of a challenge to find, but worthwhile discovering. Look for a road starting near the restrooms, and follow it for 200 feet to a path veering off to the right. You'll see the structure, an ivy-covered mystery — it's like finding an ancient tomb. Three 8-inch guns were placed here. They remained for only 2 to 3 years, when they were removed and deployed elswhere.

You can walk or bike for about three quarters of a mile along the old military access road. The road is oriented to the southwest, so sunlight lasts well into the evening on summer nights. It's paved and flat, therefore very accessible to disabled people as well. Two birding blinds are located along the water for discreet viewing of water fowl, although during the migration times in spring and fall, the real action is inland and uphill, when the place is alive with thousands of little birds en route to somewhere else.

You can reach the upper part of the fort complex by hiking up the asphalt trail near the Vinton Battery. Up there are the officers' houses, what remains of the old parade ground, as well as the former location of the famous "listening ear" antenna that helped break the Japanese code during W.W.II (See chapter on **Battlepoint Park**, page 12)

The fort's strategic location was taken seriously again during World War II when a submarine net and mine field were stretched across Rich Passage. Today, with nets and mines gone, ferry boats and Navy ships regularly ply these waters.

You can picnic at a scenic spot on the south end of the park, but you'll have to walk in along the car-less road. There is ample parking and a boat launch area inside the north entrance.

Both state parks are part of the Cascadia Marine Trail and each has a designated campsite for kayakers on the shore.

Directions:

Fay-Bainbridge Highway 305 north from Winslow to the Day Road intersection. There is a sign for the park. Turn right and continue to a "T" at Sunrise Drive. Turn left and drive about 1.4 miles to the park entrance.

Hours: 8 AM to dusk, except for campers and overnight kayakers. Campground open April 1 through mid-October.

Fort Ward Highway 305 north to High School Road. Left on High School, continue west until it ends in a "T" junction at Fletcher Bay Road. Turn left and continue until another "T" at Lynwood Center Road. Turn right and follow the road to Lynwood Center - a commercial area with Tudor-style architecture. Continue on the same road, which becomes Pleasant Beach Drive. After a bend to the left, the arterial will continue as Oddfellows Road. Keep to the right, on Pleasant Beach Drive, and you will arrive at the main entrance of the park. You can also park your car at Lynwood Center and walk the extra mile or so along the pleasant residential road for more exercise.

Hours: 8 AM to dusk, except for overnight kayakers.

Information on all Washington State parks is available at *parks.wa.gov/*

9 SUQUAMISH TRIBAL CENTER & MUSEUM

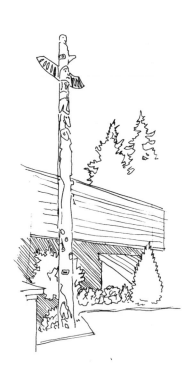

Suquamish Tribal Center & Museum

The Suquamish Tribe is recognized by the Federal government as a sovereign nation with the Tribal Center as its seat of government, located near the beach at Agate Pass. This is the southern part of the **Port Madison Indian Reservation** which centers around the towns of Suquamish and Indianola.

Adjoining the Tribal Center is the **Suquamish Museum**, a place where you can get a glimpse of the world view of the native people of this area from their own viewpoint and through their artifacts and photographs. "The Eyes of Chief

Seattle" is the premier exhibit. It received international acclaim when it traveled to Nantes, France, as part of Seattle's Sister City exchange. It tells the history of the original inhabitants of the Puget Sound as though Chief Seattle himself were your tour guide.

Chief Seattle, the city's namesake, was not only a leader of the Suquamish people, he was an orator and visionary. Actually, the native Salish language, Lushootseed, does not have a word for "chief". Tribes were guided by royalty, hereditary leaders and elders.

Sealth, or Seattle, was the hereditary leader of the Suquamish and Duwamish tribes. He lived from 1786 to 1866, and was friendly toward early settlers and intrigued by their technological ingenuity. For generations, many Native American tribes had kept slaves -- usually people from other tribes conquered in battle. But Seattle freed his own slaves when Abraham Lincoln issued the Emancipation Proclamation in 1863.

In addition to the city named for him, Seattle is known for the poignant speech he made in 1854, elaborated upon through two translations, addressing the crisis besetting his culture which was caused by European settlement.

This speech is known world-wide for its spiritual and ecological insight. You can experience it first-hand at the museum.

A replica of Old Man House is on display in the museum. The original longhouse built at the water's edge near the town of Suquamish was over 900 feet long. (See next chapter)

Another excellent audio-visual presentation shows interviews with tribal elders and their accounts of growing up in the area during times of turbulent cultural transition.

In 1993 an 11-man traditional dugout canoe, hand-carved from a huge cedar log in a shed adjacent to the museum, left the reservation on a traditional journey to Bella Bella, British Columbia. The 576-mile trip was for the Qatuwas Festival, an event strengthening unity among and between coastal waterborne tribes and bands.

The cultural heritage of this water-borne tribe is kept alive at this very active Tribal Center, which hosts crafts fairs and other activities.

An excellent display of traditional Suquamish basketry is also on display, donated from the personal collections of tribal members and tribal archives.

The Suquamish Museum was recently rated by the Smithsonian Institute as the best historical museum of Native Americans in the Northwest.

The museum bookstore has a large selection of books, many that you won't find anywhere else, about local Native Americans and their culture and history. Native art and crafts are also available.

The **Clearwater Casino,** operated by the tribe, is a gambling establishment offering the usual assortment of gaming tables as well as bingo and slot machines. Stage entertainment may include Elvis or female impersonators and a different band every weekend. A restaurant, snack bar and substantial and reasonably priced buffet are available daily.

Located just west of the Agate Pass bridge, the casino is an important part of the Suquamish Tribe's economy, employing tribal members and providing money earmarked for community uses.The new, expanded complex also offers conference facilities and a parking garage.

Directions: North on Highway 305 over the Agate Pass Bridge. Watch for the left turn lane for Sandy Hook Road. Drive approximately ½ mile.

Information:

Suquamish Tribal Center and Museum, Port Madison Indian Reservation, 15838 Sandy Hook Road, Suquamish, WA 98370, 360/598-3311, *www.suquamish.nsn.us*

Clearwater Casino, 800/375-6073, 360/598-6889, *clearwatercasino.com*

SUQUAMISH

The Grave of Chief Seattle

Suquamish can't really reveal itself to a quick drive-through tour. There is an unexpected depth and interest to this little town that unfolds to the person who takes the time to explore it.

The residents of Suquamish are proud of their town and I've heard some of them refer to it as the "last bastion of freedom". Their homes, many built on tiny lots, are imaginative and unfettered flights of self-expression and house artists, writers, craftsmen and other interesting people, both members of the Suquamish tribe as well as non-Native Americans, who lease land from the tribe.

The town is the center of the **Port Madison Indian Reservation**.

Old Man House, a waterfront park and Washington State Heritage site, is the location of what was once the largest Indian longhouse on Puget Sound and home to Chief Sealth and the Suquamish tribe. Once a tiny state park, it has finally been given back to the Suquamish tribe.

The building was between 500 and 900 feet long and 50 feet wide, with 40 "apartments" for various tribal members. The imposing structure stood until 1870 when it was demolished by the U.S. Army Corps of Engineers as a "structural nuisance". The beach is still white with the crushed shells from 500 generations of clam feasts. A shelter structure built near the beach, constructed as the longhouses were, contains a display describing the location and history of the original building.

In the center of the town stands the **totem pole** carved by Joe Hillaire, a well-known Suquamish totem pole carver. Just up the hill from the pole is St. Peter`s Catholic church, dating back to 1898 and still actively holding services.

Beyond the church is a cemetery with the unmistakable **grave of Chief Seattle** marked by well-tended war canoes mounted on cedar logs There is a path ringing the site where people walk around quietly (clockwise is the traditional practice, honoring each of the four directions), paying tribute to his memory and vision.

Once a year, during the **Chief Seattle Days** celebration at the end of August, people gather around the grave in a ceremony acknowledging this great leader. It is a beautiful ritual hosted by the tribe and attended by people of all races and creeds.

The rest of that weekend is given over to a major celebration. A huge pow-wow with songs and dances attracts indigenous people from many parts of the US and the rest of the world. Interesting booths feature handicrafts, beading supplies and tasty foods like fry bread. There are dancing and drumming competitions. For some of the dances, visitors are invited to join in. A salmon and clambake, royalty pageant and traditional canoe races make the weekend a memorable one.

All this takes place on and around what locals call "The Slab", a large paved area on the waterfront used for special occasions.

The Fourth of July is also an intense time. Many Native Americans are really enthusiastic about fireworks. They sell them legally (to be used only on the reservation) along Highway 305 in competing booths. By law, they can only be sold a few weeks before July 4th until midnight of the 4th. At that time many of the unsold fireworks are disposed of by setting them off that night - on The Slab – which is transformed by the pyrotechnic spectacle.

New Year's is another period when fireworks may be purchased and enjoyed. For the rest of the year, Suquamish is a quiet, pleasant, interesting and friendly town.

Just 4 miles north of Suquamish on Miller Bay Road at the intersection of the road to Indianola, the Suquamish Tribe operates a salmon and oyster hatchery with a unique design featured in national architectural magazines. An artesian well provides the water for the hatchery ponds, which are kept clean with a biological filtering system that also recycles the water. The tribe releases more than 5 million sockeye, chum and silver salmon every year into the Puget Sound water system. Tours of the **Grovers Creek Hatchery** are available.

Directions: From the Bainbridge Island ferry terminal in Winslow, take Highway 305 north. Cross the Agate Pass bridge and turn right at the traffic light. Continue 1.2 miles to Suquamish. Obey the speed limit. Look for signs pointing to Old Man House and Chief Seattle's grave.

Information:

Suquamish Tribal Center and Museum, Port Madison Indian Reservation, 15838 Sandy Hook Road, Suquamish, WA 98370, 360/598-3311, *suquamish.nsn.us*

Grovers Creek Fish Hatchery, Miller Bay Road at Indianola Road, 360/598-3142

Chief Seattle Days: Third weekend in August. For information contact the Suquamish Tribal Center.

POULSBO

Front Street, Poulsbo

Poulsbo, long known as "Little Norway", was settled in the 1880s by people from that country. Later more immigrants from other parts of Scandinavia settled in this area which so resembled the fjords of their native lands.

For many decades, Norwegian was the language most likely heard in the streets, but today it survives mostly in words like "lefse", "lutefisk" and "Uff Da!"*.

The town lies along the eastern shore of Liberty Bay and on its surrounding hills, and is a busy port for fishing boats, working boats and pleasure craft. Once, the Poulsbo fleet went all the way to the Bering Sea to bring back salt cod.

The town was named "Paulsbo", which is Norwegian for "Paul's Place", but because the Postmaster General misread the handwriting, the official spelling became "Poulsbo". However, everyone still persists in correctly pronouncing it "Paulsbo".

The lofty spire of the First Lutheran Church reverently crowns the hilltop just above the old town. Poulsbo is a walking town, and the whole place is a scenic treat. There are colorful and interesting shops, many featuring handwork by Scandinavian and other local craftsmen, and of course you are never far from a good restaurant or a latte. Textile enthusiasts will enjoy the quilt shop, and there are still many people carrying on the specialty Norwegian floral painting technique of "rosemaling"—an ornamental art form consisting of floral decorations with curls of base colors and swirls of highlights.

A walk along the waterfront will reveal another way of life -- those who spend their lives afloat. A small community of people live aboard boats throughout the year and many visitors arrive by boat, sightseeing the downtown area on foot.

During summer, arts and crafts shows often take place at the **Waterfront Park**, and live music often can be found at the **Kvelstad Bandstand**, as well as an occasional wedding. This is also the place to watch **Fireworks on the Fjord** every July 3. At the north end of the park take a delightful walk on the boardwalk, which parallels the eastern shore of the head of the bay -- a great place to watch for bald eagles and interesting tidal life.

Liberty Bay was originally called "Dogfish Bay" because of the dogfish-rendering operation which provided fish oils (and an apparently unforgettable accompanying olfactory experience) for greasing the logging skids in the area. Residents later insisted on the more attractive alternative, but the old name still persists in Dogfish Creek, the salmon stream at the head of the bay.

If you want to get really up-close and personal with sea life, the **Marine Science Center of the Northwest** has interesting displays of local marine creatures. The Center has close ties to local schools, and provides educational programs. The exhibits are collected by local volunteer divers and some, especially the octopuses, are returned to the wild after their brief close encounters with humans.

And if that isn't enough hands-on experience with nature, you can rent a kayak, sailboat or power boat and explore all the interesting bays and inlets of the area yourself. Public tennis courts are also located right along the shore across from the Yacht Club.

The **A. Phimister Proctor Museum** at the head of the bay in the Libery Bay Auto complex showcases a collection of exquisite sculptures—bronzes, plaster models and sketches—by the most prolific sculptor of monumental works in the US and grandfather of the proprietor.

Once a year, Poulsbovians celebrate their heritage with **Viking Fest**, a carnival with booths and food stalls, concerts in the park and a parade replete with wild Viking warriors in horned helmets. The date occurs on a weekend near May 17, Norwegian Constitution Day.

More authentically, perhaps, to celebrate the beginning of summer, Poulsbo also hosts **Midsommarfest**, a gathering of Scandinavian folk from the whole Puget Sound region, and often guest performers from Scandinavia as well. The ancient, ceremonial 55-foot *Majstang*, or Midsommar pole, is decorated with greenery and raised amidst much pomp and ceremony, with hundreds of dancers and fiddlers in colorful folk costumes in procession. Against a background of snow-capped mountains and fjord-like bays, it could make you think you were back in the old country.

Raab Park, the location of Midsommarfest, sits on a hilltop offering a spectacular view all year round.

In October, the First Lutheran Church puts on their annual **Lutefisk Dinner**, a tradition since 1913. It's your chance to taste lutefisk and other exotic Scandinavian delicacies.

*Glossary:

Lutefisk - the Viking mariners discovered that dried and salted codfish could be stored almost indefinitely, soaked in lye to reconstitute it at some later date, rinsed and soaked in fresh water to revive it further, then boiled and actually eaten.

Lefse - a potato-based version of a tortilla, often eaten with butter, sugar and cinnamon

Uff Da! - expression of mock disbelief, usually exclaimed while slapping the forehead with the heel of your hand.

Directions: **Poulsbo** is located at the junction of Highways 3 and 305. From Highway 305 at Hostmark (first traffic light), turn left and follow signs to "Historic Poulsbo".

Raab Park: From 305 turn right (east) on Hostmark, then watch for a sign pointing to the right.

Information: **Poulsbo Chamber of Commerce** 19131 8th Ave NE, 360/779-4848, *poulsbochamber.com*

Marine Science Center, downtown Poulsbo just south of Waterfront Park, 360/779-5549, *poulsbomsc.org Hours*: 11-4:30 daily except holidays, *Admission:* Adults $4, 13-17 & Seniors $3, 2-12 $2, 3rd Tuesday of each month is Free

A. Phimister Proctor Museum, 20201 Front St, call for appointment: 360/779-2574, *proctormuseum.org*

It may seem a little out of the ordinary to include a food market in a tour guide, but this is no ordinary market. Not only is it in a handy location for picking up a quick snack on your way to the Olympics, it's a great place to stop and browse.

Central Market is a store where you can buy a plate of fresh sushi or a bale of hay, a slice of pizza or a bouquet of flowers. On a nice day you can sit on the terrace with a cappuccino and Danish and chat with the locals.

It was envisioned as a "destination market", and that is what it has become, attracting people from the northern part of Kitsap County to shop and socialize, as well as lucky travelers who stop and look around. It serves our multi-ethnic population with a wide variety of foods and items not found in the average supermarket.

It is not uncommon to see a busload of Japanese grocers touring the store, sent by their firms back home to study American retailing practices.

There is a strong pan-Asian accent in the food selection, with not only imported prepared and frozen items, but also fresh fruits, vegetables and

sea creatures you may never have encountered before in a produce or seafood department. (We once saw a 65–pound octopus on a large bed of ice. It was completely gone, sold piece by piece, in two days.) In-house sushi chefs maintain a constant supply of ready-to-eat delicacies.

The natural foods department rivals many a health food co-op, and you can chop off a chunk of homemade soap in any size that will meet your needs. Organic produce from local growers is featured in season.

This concept was the creation of Town & Country Market, Inc. (T&C) based on Bainbridge Island and owned by the Nakata and Loverich families who have lived there since the early 1900s.

During the outbreak of W.W.II, one of the Nakata sons, Mo, entered the Army and served with the highly decorated 100th Battalion, 442nd Regiment in Italy and France. He returned to Bainbridge Island in 1945, and in 1947, with his best friend, Ed Loverich, opened a small grocery at the center of the island where Bainbridge Gardens stands today (See Chapter 5).

T&C was formed in 1957, when Mo and Ed with Mo's brother, John, who had a store in Winslow, closed both stores, and built their first "big" store downtown, which still flourishes as the **Town & Country Market**. (It warrants a separate visit when you are in Winslow, Chapter 3: check out the extensive deli selections and the kitchen & wine shop on the lower level.)

The company now owns three stores in Kitsap County and three on the Seattle side.

Central Market opened in 1995. Much environmental consciousness went into the planning for its construction and ongoing operation. Recycled materials and energy-efficient systems were used whenever possible.

Today, there are several generations of the Nakata and Loverich families working in the company helping to keep things running smoothly. You get the impression that all the other employees are part of the extended family, as well.

In keeping with its environmental policies, Central Market has encouraged its customers to use recycled paper or plastic shopping bags, and currently sells a shopping bag made from recycled pop bottles, complete with the store's logo. Over the years they have encouraged customers to take their Central Market shopping bags with them as they travel the world, and an entire wall near the main entrance displays many photos documenting the far-flung destinations these shopping bags have attained.

Little Valley and Big Valley Roads

Little Valley Road is the beginning of the scenic backdoor route to the Hood Canal floating bridge. Take Little Valley Road north from Central Market along its winding course through picturesque farm land until you come to Bond Road (mind the speed bumps). Cross Bond Road (carefully, the traffic can be a little scary) and Little Valley Road becomes Big Valley Road. This drive through pleasant rolling farms is scenic in any season.

Along the route are the **Manor Farm Inn**, a working farm as well as a lovely bed and breakfast in a perfect setting, where you may see people training Scottish sheep dogs if you're lucky; **Molly Ward Gardens**, whose owners craft creative dried flower arrangements from their delightful cottage garden as well as tasty meals; and the **Llama Rose Farm**, where Winifred Whitfield, once a high-powered financial adviser on Wall Street, left the rat race and has devoted herself full time to raising llamas and developing her farm and garden activities. At last report, she had a herd of llamas, a dromedary and a Bactrian camel.

Manor Farm Inn and Llama Rose Farm are both popular spots for weddings.

When Big Valley Road ends at Highway 3, take a right and the Hood Canal floating bridge is just a few more miles.

Directions: From Highway 305 you can see the market plainly on the right two traffic lights north of the main Poulsbo intersection at Hostmark Street. Central Market is at the intersection of Little Valley Road and the highway.

Information:
Central Market: 360/779-1881, *Hours:* 24/7
Manor Farm Inn: 26069 Big Valley Rd. 360/779-4628, *manorfarminn.com*
Molly Ward Gardens: 27462 Big Valley Rd, 360/779-4471, *mollywardgardens.com*
Llama Rose Farm, 27248 Big Valley Rd, 360/779-1375, *llamarose.com*

13   HOOD CANAL BRIDGE

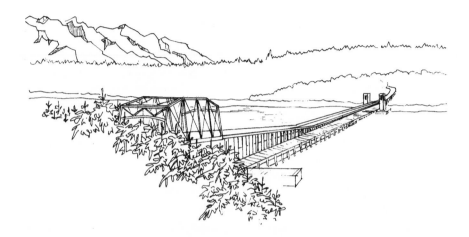

The original **Hood Canal Floating Bridge** was built in 1961, and at the time was the largest floating concrete structure on tidal water in the world. It also has the longest draw span ever constructed. The part of the bridge which floats is 6,470 feet long. The portion of the roadways at either end act as giant hinges which swing up and down up to 15 feet twice a day with the tides.

The bridge was a boon to the economy of the Olympic Peninsula until a giagantic storm washed it away on February 13, 1979. To get an idea of the magnitude of the waves, the observation tower near the center of the bridge was skewered by a giant log, right through its windows.

The last person who tried to drive across was a semi truck driver, who, upon seeing the seriousness of the situation, tried to back off the bridge. His empty trailer acted as a giant sail, forcing him to slam repeatedly into the lee rail and causing him further anguish.

After successfully maneuvering to safety at last, he watched the bridge blow away right before his eyes. Fortunately there were no fatalities. The bridge was totally destroyed, and still lies nearby at the bottom of the 250-foot-deep Hood Canal.

The present bridge is of a modified design, reconstructed with engineering enhancements to make sure such a disaster never happens again. It's interesting to note that a submarine-proof net is suspended underwater across the opening to Hood Canal - to guard Naval Subase Bangor to the south.

Today the bridge is much safer and as scenic as ever. To the west are the snow-clad Olympic Mountains, and nearby to the north is the sometime island, Hood's Head. On a clear day you can see distant Mount Baker to the northeast, a volcanic peak in the Cascades near the Canadian border.

If you park at the east end of the bridge and walk along the north side, you can reach the secret area below the bridge deck where local people come to fish. Fish-cleaning stations have even been thoughtfully provided.

On the western side of the bridge to the north of the highway is **Shine Tidelands State Park**, a public tidelands. Clamming is permitted in season as long as there isn't a "red tide" warning. (This toxic organism occurs during red algae blooms and can be deadly to humans eating contaminated shellfish.)

When the tide is out you can walk over the causeway to **Hood's Head**, once known as "Whiskey Spit", according to local legends a transfer point for illegal spirits from Canada during Prohibition. (Just check a tide table to make sure you can get back!)

This road, a backdoor route to Port Townsend, will also take you to **Port Ludlow**, once the sister sawmill to Port Gamble and now a conference center and retirement community featuring a 27-hole **golf course** designed by Robert Muir Graves (open to the public) with views and vistas that can only be imagined in landlocked parts of the world.

Keep your eyes alert for sightings of sea lions, harbor seals and bald eagles. Migrating gray whales and pods of Orcas also often visit these waters. Nuclear submarines from the nearby Trident missile base at Bangor must pass through the draw span to have access to the ocean. Often traffic is held up and the draw span opened, providing a fine photo opportunity to those who leave their cars for a close-up view of the subs and their awesome bow waves.

An electronic signboard along Highway 305 near Central Market in Poulsbo displays traffic alerts about the bridge.

Directions: Take Highway 305 north to junction with Highway 3, go north to Hood Canal Bridge

Information: The Hood Canal bridge is sometimes closed during severe winds and high seas. Call 800/419-9085 for the latest updates.

Clamming is not OK when the toxic "red tide" algae is flourishing. Check the Recreational Shellfish Hotline 800/562-5632 or Washington State Dept. of Fish & Wildlife 360/249-4628, *ww4.doh.wa.gov/gis/biotoxin.htm*

The Resort at Ludlow Bay, 200 Olympia Pl, 800/732-1239, 360/437-2222 Tee time reservations 800/455-0272, *portludlowresort.com*

Port Ludlow Golf Club, 800/455-0272, *portludlowresort.com*

Be Advised: The Hood Canal Bridge will be closed for repairs for approximately eight weeks starting in May 2007. More info at www.hoodcanalbridge.com

St. Paul's Episcopal Church

Step into another era when you visit this charming 19th century mill town. The town has remained intact since its founding due to the fact that it was entirely owned by the Puget Mill Company, a partnership under Pope & Talbot of San Francisco, to house and accommodate its workers and their families. Port Gamble was home to the longest continuously operated mill operation in North America. The mill finally closed in 1995, but the original buildings in the town still stand, perfectly preserved, a time capsule set in a pristine, scenic setting.

It's no coincidence that the town has a definite New England appearance. The mill founders, Captain William Talbot and Andrew J. Pope, were from East Machias, Maine, and the architectural style reflects that of their hometown. When they arrived in 1853 they immediately set about building a sawmill, and by 1858 there was a school, a church, a store and a population of 326 people. The early settlers brought East Coast elm trees and even *dandelion seeds* to remind them of home. (So *that's* where they came from!)

There seemed to be an endless supply of fir, hemlock and cedar to saw up into dimension lumber, which was shipped from Port Gamble all over the planet —to the diamond mines of South Africa, the new cities of Australia and New Zealand, and in 1906 used to rebuild San Francisco after the earthquake and fire. During World War I, the mill supplied lumber to the allies of America, from Europe to Africa.

In the mid 1960s, Pope & Talbot saw a rare opportunity to protect and preserve this small part of the past for future generations. They restored and rebuilt 30 houses and buildings, located utilities underground and installed gas street lamps as they had been in the past. In 1966 Port Gamble was designated a National Historic Site.

Earlier, the **Port Gamble Cemetery** had been designated a National Historic Landmark, because in 1856, Gustave Englebrecht, a coxswain on the battleship *Massachusetts*, was fatally wounded by a bullet from a local indigenous person, thereby becoming the first Euro-American casualty in the Pacific. A plaque near his grave commemorates this bit of history. We can't resist taking a walk in the cemetery whenever we visit Port Gamble. High on a hilltop overlooking Admiralty Inlet, the view and the atmosphere are scenic and serene.

By the 1920s, the big lumber boom was winding down, and Port Gamble's distance from transcontinental rail lines further put it at a disadvantage. The mill was sold and reacquired by Pope & Talbot, and continued to operate on a small scale until November 30, 1995, when the mill whistle blew for the last time and the mill closed.

Today the most popular place in town is the **General Store**, looking exactly the way it did 150 years ago. While it no longer carries some of the staples that it did before the mill closed and is now more geared to visitors, a supreme effort is made to offer old-timey items and many things you won't find in the average souvenir store. Snack foods such as ice cream, and the ubiquitous latte are also available.

The store has a three-sided mezzanine which houses the **"Of Sea and Shore" Museum** of sea shells from around the world. Possibly the largest private collection, only a fraction of the 25,000 species are on display at any one time. A related book shop is located downstairs.

Don't leave Port Gamble without a visit to the excellent **Historical Museum** behind and below the general store. Artifacts from Port Gamble's past are arranged in well-designed displays of a quality that you might never expect in such an out-of-the-way small town. There is a full-size replica of Captain Talbot's quarters on the brig *Oriental*, complete with the original ship's log. A saw filing exhibit displays the tools used to keep the mill's blades sharp. Rooms from two buildings which no longer exist, the elegant Puget Hotel and Admiralty Hall, the fine mansion which was home to the mill's general manager, Cyrus Walker, are recreated with original and period furnishings. And a Native American long house is also featured, built of cedar boards and furnished with finely crafted mats and baskets.

No visit to the town is complete without seeing **St. Paul's Episcopal Church**, an exact duplicate of one in East Machias, Maine, which reminds us of those we've seen in Currier and Ives prints. It's a

popular place for weddings, and holds regular services on Sundays.

The **Kitsap Peninsula Visitor and Convention Bureau** is located right next to the general store. You can stop in and chat with volunteers and pick up maps, brochures and other information about the area.

A **Medieval Faire**, hosted by the Society for Creative Anachronism, takes place at Port Gamble in late spring. Merchants supply everything from the perfect touch for your costume to historical weapons. Archery tournaments and jousting competitions provide an opportunity to shout "Huzzah" for your favorite knight.

Directions: From Hansville: South to Country Corners intersection and turn right (west) on Hwy 104. At the next traffic light, turn right following Hwy104 and continue 4 miles.

From Poulsbo: Take Bond Road (Hwy 307) to the traffic light at Hwy104. Turn left on 104 and continue 4 miles.

From the Hood Canal Bridge: Turn left on Hwy. 104 and continue 1 mile.

Information:

Kitsap Peninsula Visitor and Convention Bureau 360/297-8200, *visitkitsap.com. Hours:* Visitor Information Center: 9-5 daily in summer, less on weekends in winter

Port Gamble General Store 360/297-7636, *Hours:* 8:00-5:00 daily except Christmas & New Year's. *ofseaandshore.com*

Port Gamble Historic Museum 360/297-8074 *Hours:* May 1-Oct 31, 10:30-5 daily, winter season by appointment. *Admission:* Adults $2.50, Students/Seniors $1.50, kids under 6 free.

St. Paul's Episcopal Church, 360/297-3800, Services: 8:30 AM every Sunday.

The Old Kingston Hotel

Indianola

Indianola is a tiny settlement at the end of a two and a half mile road off Miller Bay Road. It is best known for its beach and long dock over Puget Sound, providing anglers a constant opportunity, swimmers a 30-foot dive, and sand engineers a site for the annual Sand Castle Building Competition during Indianola Days in late July or early August.

Indianola was originally developed and marketed as a summer home area for Seattle inhabitants. It has one of the finest sandy beaches on Puget Sound (hence the sand castle contest).

The dock at Indianola was built to accommodate the "Mosquito Fleet" steamers (see Chapter 2, page 6).

Indianola's everything store, the Indianola Country Store & Deli, built in the 1930s, supplies the local residents with just about everything they need, from butter and eggs to video rentals.

Kingston

The sleepy but slowly growing little town of Kingston, about 15 miles north of Bainbridge Island, is the second major gateway to the Kitsap and Olympic Peninsulas. The Kingston ferry comes from Edmonds, just north of Seattle, and the Kingston vessels hold considerably fewer cars than those of the Bainbridge run. A passenger-only commuter ferry to downtown Seattle is coming in the near future.

Like most small towns in America, the commercial area of Kingston exists almost exclusively to meet the needs of the local residents, with a supermarket, lumberyard (the finest in the county), feed and garden store, veterinary clinic, real estate offices, etc. However, there are a few hidden gems here for the traveller as well, some in walking distance from the ferry.

The first hidden gem is Kim McElroy's **Spirit of Horse Gallery**, open by appointment, preferably with a week's advance notice. Kim is a nationally- known equine artist whose paintings range from commissioned portraits of real horses to mystical portrayals from other dimensions, all demonstrating her exceptionable ability to definitively capture the "spirt of horse".

The second gem is Dan Hinkley's **Heronswood Nursery**, known for many years to serious plant collectors for its vast offerings of unusual perennials and shrubs and recently catapulted to national stardom by Martha Stewart. Again, local zoning laws make it an "appointment only" option. Shopping appointments can be made pretty much any weekday except during the extreme spring shipping period from March 9 through May 18. Even so, visitors may make appointments to shop on Saturdays during the that time. There are also several Garden Open days and nursery sales during the year.

The third unexpected jewel is the **Kingston Classic Cycling Museum**, located in the historic Kingston Hotel. Here you will find bicycles important in American cycling history, vintage racing gear and other memorabilia. The shop sells new bikes and equipment as well.

There are 40 guest slips at the Kingston marina on Appletree Cove, making it a destination for watercraft other than ferries.

There is also food. The **Kingston Inn** has a dining room with a fine reputation and the **Restaurant at the Dock** has steaks, seafood and outdoor dining on the waterfront, as well as live music and dancing Fridays and Saturdays.

Kingston was originally a lumber town and settlement of farmers, growing strawberries, lettuce and orchard fruits. There was a University Outing Camp from the U-Dub (University of Washington) located there until 1933.

Kingston has a weekly **Farmers' Market** on Saturdays, mid-May until October, and hosts a Blue Grass Festival in September, and a Country Christmas event in December.

The Fourth of July is a major festival in Kingston, complete with parade, fireworks and other activities, but the most interesting feature is the transformation of Kola Kole Park into "Tiny Town", with a miniature model of downtown Kingston, as well as games and rides.

Kingston, like Bainbridge Island, possesses a new skate park for skateboarders and in-line skaters, also designed by professionals.

Directions: To Indianola: Hwy 305 on Bainbridge, right on thte Suquamish Road, through Suquamish north on Miller Bay Road, right at Grover's Creek Hatchery on Indianola Road.

To Kingston: Highway 305 north, turn right on Suquamish Road, go through Suquamish and continue on Miller Bay to Hwy 104 (Kountry Korners or George's Corner), right to Kingston.

Information:

Indianola Country Store & Deli, 360/297-3327

Kingston Chamber of Commerce, 11212 Hwy 104, 360/297-3813, *kingstonchamber.org*

Kingston Classic Cycling Museum, 25931 NE Washington Blvd, 360/297-7144 *kingstonclassiccycle.com*

Kingston Inn, 24886 Washington Blvd, 360/297-3373

Kingston Marina, Port of Kingston, 360/2997-3545

The Restaurant at the Dock, 25864 Washington Blvd, 360/297-8566

Spirit of Horse Gallery, 800/842-1123, 360/297-7736, *spiritofhorse.com*

Heronswood Nursery, 7530 NE 288th St., Kingston, WA 98346, 360/297-4172, *heronswood.com*

This little lighthouse, the very first on Puget Sound, has been operational since 1879. Its fresnel lens and light are the original ones installed. Visible for 15 miles, its light has been guiding ships, ferries and pleasure craft for more than 120 years. In 1900, a foghorn, which is still operational, was added to the complex. The lighthouse is not very tall, but because of its location on the beach it is easily visible. Like many other lighthouses in the world, it has been automated and no longer houses a keeper and his family.

Point No Point was given this curious name by Vancouver, who observed that the point was visible from some directions and not from others.

The surrounding area is very scenic. As you approach on the highway you will arrive at the crest of a hill with a sweeping view of Admiralty Inlet and the mountains beyond. The next road to the right takes you to the lighthouse. The beach is a pleasant walk, but before you go wading out too far, be aware that there is an abrupt 100-foot deep drop-off close to the shore, which is bad news for waders but good news for anglers, as it

has created an almost legendary fishing spot. As the tide goes out, a giant eddy is created, trapping millions of bait fish for salmon to snack on. Then this, of course, attracts fisherman to catch the salmon right from the shore. Sometimes it is as entertaining to watch the fishing as it is to take part in it. The point has the reputation of being one of the premier saltwater fly casting areas on Puget Sound.

A second approach to the lighthouse is available to those willing to hike a bit. A tiny parking area with a sign **"Point No Point County Park"** offers a pleasant hike through the woods, and along the sand dune bluffs and shore to the lighthouse. But the return trip up that hill (complete with built-in steps) is not for the faint-hearted.

If you are a dedicated bird-watcher, be sure to bring your binoculars and camera. There are often birding trips organized to see the more than 50 species that frequent the area.

If you like to collect driftwood, it would be worthwhile to continue on the highway through **Hansville** along Twin Spits Road to **Foulweather**

Bluff. There, near a cluster of cottages and resorts, find a place to park along the road end and hike to the beach, which has an enormous pile of driftwood above the high tide line. Be careful to time the tide carefully, so you don't get cut off from a dry return. It's a good idea to pack a lunch to snack on while sunning yourself on a pile of driftwood.

A mile before the end of the road is a **Nature Conservancy trail** which will take you directly to the beach to the south. This is a real challenge to find, as the sign is not on the road but up the trail, but is well worth the effort. A little sleuth work can lead you to an obvious trail on the south side of the road. Exactly 3.0 miles from the Hansville grocery store is a parking area between two signs. The short forest trail follows the edge of a saltwater marsh and leads to a wide beach with sandstone cliffs. Low tide exposes a rock and gravel shelf with tide pools. Most local people know about this trail through word of mouth, so it has fairly light use. This 100-acre reserve abounds with fox, otter, raccoon and deer, and many marsh birds, so please do not bring a dog on the trail, even on leash. Camping, fires and clamming are also not allowed.

Directions:
Point No Point Lighthouse - Main Driving Route: North on Hansville Road 6 miles from the Country Corners intersection (Highway 104). When you reach the crest of a hill with a sweeping view of the Sound, take the next right turn on Point No Point Road.

Point No Point Lighthouse - Hiking Route: North on Hansville Road to Gus Halvor Road. Turn right (east) and follow the road to the parking area for Point No Point County Park trail head.

Foulweather Beach: go back to the main Hansville highway and continue north, through the little resort town of Hansville, follow its turn to the west as it changes names to Twin Spits Road and dead ends some four miles further at the driftwood beach road end.

Nature Conservancy trail: On the south side of the road 3.0 miles from the Hansville grocery store and one mile before the road end is the entrance to the trail.

Information:
Point No Point Lighthouse, 360/337-5350, Tours April 13 through September 29, Saturdays and Sundays 12 to 4 PM

Foulweather Bluff Preserve, *nature.org/ wherewework/northamerica/states/washington/ preserves/art6363.html*

Point No Point Casino, 7989 Salish Lane NE, (Off the Hansville Rd on the Port Gamble S'Kallam Reservation), 866/547-6468, 360/297-0070 *pointnopointcasino.com*

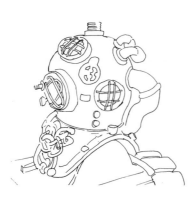

Ron's earliest recollection of Keyport was viewing it from Bainbridge Island across Port Orchard Bay back in the sixties. Keyport's deep water port provided an ideal place for a US Navy torpedo testing station. From time to time a small boat with a rotating yellow light and a siren would alert people to the fact that testing was about to begin. He remembers that, on several occasions, an unarmed torpedo would wash up on a neighbor's beach. One stray torpedo actually blew up the boathouse of former Washington Secretary of State Ralph Munro.

Like many local people everywhere who are oblivious to the attractions around them, only recently did we decide to drive around the bay and check out the base. We were pleasantly surprised to discover a world-class museum specializing in undersea technology, naval history and marine science, with only a secondary emphasis on torpedo technology. It boasts the largest collection of undersea objects in the United States in 20,000 square feet of exhibits.

After being welcomed by friendly and helpful volunteer docents, you can wander through the many well-designed and educational displays of diving equipment, underwater exploration and large-scale models of oil rigs and submarines. There is even an actual WWII Japanese one-man suicide submarine - no more than a manually-operated torpedo - that really gave us the creeps.

Also inside is the Alvin, the deep-sea diving sub that was used to recover the hydrogen bomb lost off the coast of Spain and later assisted in the search for the Titanic.

Outdoors, next to the parking lot, can be seen the *Trieste*, the diving vehicle that made the deepest descent in history into the Marianas Trench in the Pacific Ocean, and the *Sub-Human II*, the two-man human powered sub that got into the Guinness Book of Records by setting a world speed record.

Adjoining the display area is a gift shop with a unique specialty: almost all the gifts, toys, books and souvenirs have a marine or underwater theme.

In addition there is a 200-seat auditorium, offering educational programs for students and a quarterly Distinguished Speakers series.

Directions: Take Route 305 north to its intersection with Highway 3, then turn south on Highway 3 to Route 308. Turn left (east) on Route 308 and follow the signs to Keyport and the museum.

Information:
Garnett Way, Keyport, 360/396-4148
keyportmuseum.cnrnw.navy.mil
Open from 10:00 AM to 4 PM daily June through September, closed Tuesdays October through May. Admission is free, donations are appreciated. (Real value for your tax dollars!)

SUBASE BANGOR (The Trident Base)

Submarine Base Bangor (Subase Bangor), known locally as "The Trident Base", fairly dominates the Kitsap Peninsula's western shore, covering 4 ½ miles of shoreline and a total of more than 7,000 acres. The population of the base is around 5,000, which includes active duty personnel and their families. It employs 11,000 military and civilian personnel and is the largest employer in Kitsap County. The base has now been renamed as part of the newly designated **Naval Base Kitsap.**

The mission of the base is to support the Trident nuclear submarines and their ballistic missiles systems, and to operate facilities for administration and personnel support.

At the heart of the base are rows of bunkers which contain enough nuclear warheads to wipe out a major country. This area is brilliantly lit at night and reflects a rosy glow off the clouds which often cover our skies. A restricted area, it is heavily guarded against trespassers.

The core of the base is surrounded by a pristine wilderness abounding with wildlife, and the base has an active environmental program, employing foresters and biologists.

Subase (pronounced "sub base") Bangor is a virtual city unto itself, with stores, health clubs, gas stations, RV rentals, all tax-free to the military personnel, as well as schools and clean, modern housing. It is strangely without advertising, billboards and attention-grabbing neon signs — for many, an ideal environment to raise a family. In 2002 Bangor was voted the world's best Naval base by readers of the *Navy Times*.

There is a small lake on the base, known as Devil's Lake, where the residents can rent a boat and go fishing. We were told by an Indian elder that, well before the coming of the Navy, Native people considered the lake an evil place with a monster living in it, and that the lake had no bottom.

Intrigued, we inquired about this and found that the story was not upheld by the Navy, who claimed to have found the bottom. But they offered no comments about the monster.

Free public tours of the base facilities and a submarine (if available) have been offered in the past. These have been very popular and are generally booked many months in advance. In addition, visitors must pass the stringent security requirements.

Military personnel, both active and retired, and their dependents as long as they have a valid ID card, have been able to visit the base along with its support facilities in the past. The events of September 2001 have made tighter security a very high priority. Check with the Public Affairs Office for the current status.

Directions: Highway 3 near Silverdale at several well-marked exits. The people arranging tours can tell you which entrance to use.

Information: Tour requests can be made through the Public Affairs Office (360) 396-4843, *nbk.navy.mil*

SILVERDALE & SEABECK

Kitsap Mall

Sometimes, even when visiting from across the country, you have a compulsion to do some "mall prowling". Quaint, friendly local shops just won't do -- it has to be the bustle of people, vast parking lots, neon lights, the fragrant smell of perfume counters and food courts. Then **Silverdale** is the place for you.

Every franchise restaurant and chain store in America is represented in this picturesque valley, like Xanadu of old, a fantasy of retail pleasures. There are also an amazing number of family-run ethnic restaurants, including a large representation of Asian cuisines.

People who live on this side of the Sound now shop here for things which used to require a long boat ride to Seattle, although the nearby location of the Trident Submarine Navy base probably had a lot to do with the choice of location for the sprawling retail area. The base may be a city unto itself (See Chapter 18), but the sailors and their dependents appreciate having a choice of places to go shopping.

The first-time visitor to Silverdale must wonder if there are actually any people who live there--it seems to be all retail stores and parking lots. Most of the inhabitants live in scenic hilltop homes or apartments with stirring views of the nearby mountains, or they live around the shores of Sinclair Inlet, an arm of Puget Sound. You can spot some of the local young people executing kickflips and ollies at the **skate board park** on Silverdale Way.

For all the bustling capitalistic activity, you just have to stop now and then to look at the ever-present snow-capped Olympic Mountains, visible almost everywhere you go, and at the view of Mount Rainier looming dramatically across Sinclair Inlet.

Silverdale's orginal settlers wanted to call it "Goldendale", but that name had already been preempted by folks along the Columbia River, so they settled for the second-most-precious metal.

Old Silverdale has almost been swallowed up by the mega building boom of the past 20 years, but in its very heart is Waterfront Park, a very nice and even romantic place to stroll along the floating piers and savor a quiet space apart from the consumer frenzy.

For a completely opposite experience, drive over to the quiet resort community of **Seabeck**, on the eastern shore of the Hood Canal.

Named "Sca-bock Harbor" by Wilkes, the original lumbermill settlement was larger than

Seattle in 1858. As in the case of Poulsbo, the name was misrecorded as "Seabeck". Seabeck was an important port for passengers as well as timber, and the shipyard run by the mill company built some of the fastest sailing ships on the West Coast, including the *Olympus*, the largest single-decked sailing ship ever built.

In contrast to its current peaceful state, early Seabeck was called "The Liveliest Town on Puget Sound" and known for bootleggers, rumrunners and saloons that were open 24/7. The cookhouse feeding the men at the mill generated so much garbage that pigs were encouraged to run through the streets to clean it up.

A log-float once ferried passengers precariously between Seabeck and Brinnon. It was eventually replaced by a small steam ferry which ran until 1941.

Both the mill and shipyard were destroyed by fire in 1886 and, rather than rebuild, the owners bought the Port Hadlock mill. Most of the townspeople followed them.

The **Seabeck Christian Conference Center** was built in 1914 as an interdenomininational conference center and campground for area churches. Parts of the original complex burned down over the years and other buildings replaced them. There are still a number of historical buildings. The conference center provides lodging and meeting room facilities to non-profit organizations and charitable institutions only. It is located across the old log pond from the **Seabeck General Store** and **cafe**.

A local entrepreneur has created the successful **Seabeck Pizza**, with several locations, with the distinction of delivering by car and *by boat*.

Scenic Beach State Park, located a short drive just south of the town center, features spectacular views of the Hood Canal and Olympic Mountains from the picnic area and beach below. There is also a campground (no RV hookups), and a historic Craftsman home which can be rented for weddings and other events.

Miami Beach, just south of Misery Point, was a sacred burial ground for the native people.

Guillemot Cove Nature Reserve offers a one-mile trail to the beach and other trails through 164 acres of varied habitat.

You can keep driving south and make a loop around the Tahuya Peninsula for more gorgeous views of the Hood Canal.

Silverdale
Directions: Two exits from Highway 3
Information: **Silverdale Chamber of Commerce** 360/692-6800, info@silverdalechamber.com
silverdalechamber.com
shopkitsapmall.com

Seabeck
Directions:
Highway 305 from Bainbridge Island through Poulsbo onto Highway 3 southbound. Take Highway 3 to the Newberry Hill Road exit. Turn west on Seabeck Hwy. Drive six miles, following signs to Seabeck.
Information:
Barbie's Seabeck Bay Cafe, 15384 Seabeck Hwy NW, 360/830-5532 Breakfast to 5 pm
Seabeck Christian Conference Center, 15395 Seabeck Hwy NW, 360/830-5010, *seabeck.org*
Seabeck General Store, 15384 Seabeck Hwy NW, 360/830-5190
Seabeck Pizza,15376 Seabeck Hwy N, 360/830-4839
Scenic Beach State Park, Ranger Station 360/830-5079, *parks.wa.gov*
Directions: In Seabeck, drive south past the bay and turn right on Scenic Beach Rd. Drive one mile to park.
Guillamot Cove Nature Reserve
Directions: Take Scenic Beach Rd to Stavis Bay Rd, a left turn shortly before the park entrance. Drive 4.5 miles and watch for the sign and parking area.

20

BREMERTON

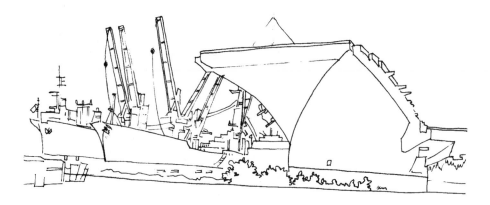

Puget Sound Naval Shipyard

In 1891, Mr. Bremer had managed to acquire some choice real estate which had not only a magnificent view of the Olympic Mountains, but also a bay that would make an excellent deep water harbor in a well-protected spot with access to the Puget Sound and the Pacific Ocean. He brought this to the attention of the US Navy. The Navy agreed with his analysis and the **Puget Sound Naval Shipyard** was born.

The Navy came first, with the shipyard. The town was built around it. The town would really prosper every time a ship arrived, full of sailors greeting their dependents. When the ship left for duty, things would quiet down a lot. Sometimes the ship would be an aircraft carrier, itself carrying the population of an entire small town. Despite the wild fluctuations this caused in the local economy, a thriving community was built.

Then in 1975, the town was devastated when the major retail community left town, joining the mall complex development of Silverdale, which was closer to the Trident submarine base, the newest center of population and economy in Kitsap County.

But out of every calamity a new opportunity is bound to appear. Generous grants from Microsoft billionaires Bill Gates (his grandfather owned a furniture store in Bremerton) and Paul Allen enabled the restoration of the old **Admiral Theater** into a first-class performing arts facility, providing a venue for Bremerton's symphony and dance company, as well as concerts, films and conferences. The boost that the city needed had begun.

Nationally-recognized artist **Amy Burnett** established the largest fine art gallery in the Northwest right in the downtown area. Other art galleries followed, and artists, eager to take advantage of the low rents, came to Bremerton.

Now with the community's new optimism and energy, the city is attracting national attention. In 1990 Money magazine chose Bremerton as the number one place to live, and Reader's Digest in 1997 rated it the fourth best place to raise a family.

Speaking of families, a fun place to visit with kids is the **Aurora Valentinetti Puppet Museum,** where you can see theatrical puppets from many different cultures and countries. The puppets sometimes appear in performances in conjunction with the **Evergreen Children's Theater.**

The new **Kitsap Conference Center** and **Bremerton Harborside** complex are due to open in the summer of 2004. Waterfront hotels, restaurants, and shops will round out the experience of conference-goers. A new public marina will be near the ferry dock, and the new City Hall will also locate there.

Although not an obvious tourist destination, Bremerton has several interesting things to offer, especially if the Navy is in your blood. You'll thrill to the sight of almost two solid shoreline miles of shipyards, filled with an incredible number and assortment of naval ships -- modern aircraft carriers, battleships, nuclear subs -- whatever happens to be there for maintenance at the time – as well as the mothball fleet of historic ships.

For many years the city was the home port of the *USS Missouri*, the World War II battleship which drew tourists from far and near. However, this ship, upon whose decks the Japanese surrender was formalized, was recently relocated to a permanent and fitting location at Pearl Harbor in Honolulu, Hawaii.

Nowadays you can tour the fully-restored Navy destroyer, ***USS Turner Joy***, which served in the Vietnam War and is permanently berthed at the waterfront park boardwalk, next to the ferry terminal. The ship is open for a small admission charge from Memorial Day to Labor Day. Near the *Turner Joy* is the **Bremerton Naval Museum,**

established for the purpose of depicting and preserving the history of the US Navy, with particular focus on the Puget Sound Naval Shipyard. They have an impressive collection of large scale models of Naval vessels. The museum will soon be moving to a new and more spacious location nearby on the waterfront. The shipyard is now part of the newly designated **Naval Base Kitsap.**

Tours of the harbor and the mothball fleet are available through **Kitsap Harbor Tours.**

For more background on Bremerton and the Kitsap Peninsula, visit the **Kitsap County Historical Society Museum** on Fourth Street.

Directions: Hwy 3 south to Kitsap Way exit, east to downtown Bremerton waterfront and shipyards.

Information:

Bremerton Area Chamber of Commerce, 360/479-3579, 301 Pacific Ave, *bremertonchamber.org*

Admiral Theater, 515 Pacific Ave, 360/373-6743, *admiraltheatre.org*

Amy Burnett Gallery, 412 Pacific Ave , 360/373-3187, *amyburnett.com*

Aurora Valentinetti Puppet Museum, 257 Fourth St, 360/373-2992

Evergreen Children's Theater, 249 Fourth St, 360/373-2992

Bremerton Naval Museum, 360/479-7447, 130 Washington, Sunday 1 to 5 and Monday thru Saturday 10 to 5. From Labor Day to Memorial Day, closed Monday. Admission free.

USS Turner Joy, Bremerton Historical Ships Association, 360/792-2457, 300 Washington Beach Avenue, Hours 10-5, Adults $5, Seniors $4, Teens $3, Kids under 5 free. *maritime.org/hnsa-dd951.htm*

Kitsap Conference Center at Bremerton Harborside, 360/377-3785, *kistapconferencecenter.com*

Kitsap County Historical Society Museum, 280 Fourth St, 360/479-6226, *waynes.net/kchsm*

Kitsap Harbor Tours, 360/377-8924, 360/876-1260

Elandan Gardens is created not only for the Gardener, but also for the Dreamer, the Believer in Fables, the Seeker of Antiquity, and the Romantic.

Seemingly random groupings of trees, sculptures and stones slowly reveal themselves as being deliberately and lovingly planned. The forests, mountains and water of the surrounding natural environment seem especially enchanting when viewed through the garden's venerable trees and rocks. Unexpected sculptures emerge from the ground like remnants of an ancient civilization.

All of this is the dedicated life work of Dan Robinson. The name "Elandan" is created by combining the French word *elan* ("courage, action, impetuous passion") and his first name.

Dan's passion is the gentle and patient art of *bonsai*, the traditional Japanese and Chinese practice of growing miniature trees. While some of Dan's specimens have been grown from seed or cuttings in the more usual manner of *bonsai* cultivation, he has also been collecting special trees from forests and mountain tops across the continents of the world for decades. Several *hundred* are on display.

The outer public garden includes plantings, sculptures, impressive rock formations with miniature trees tucked into the cracks, and a sweeping lawn to the shore of Sinclair Inlet. And then, for a very small fee, you can enter the inner sanctum, the private *bonsai* collection.

The 5-acre strolling garden is a magical experience, carefully landscaped to resemble the native original locations of the uniquely shaped, gnarled and aged trees, some as old as 1500 years. All are discreetly labeled to reveal their species, age, history and place of origin. A number of interesting Rhododendron and Japanese maple varieties are also featured.

Sculpture-like groupings of rocks are imaginatively arranged to evoke images of mysterious and exotic lands. You will see things that remind you of the stone circles and dolmens of Britain, the idols of the Pacific Islands, the ruins of Mesoamerican cultures.

It's hard to believe that this very special experience was once a landfill and log dump. It obviously took a person with imagination, intention and a lot of hard work to create this remarkable place. Many of the sculptures and pottery were created by Dan and his son, William. Three generations of Robinsons have contributed, along with Dan's wife and business partner, Diane, to make Elandan a reality.

The Gallery, considered "One of the ten best stores in the country" by *Country Living Magazine*, is a gift shop with an eclectic and tasteful collection of unique gift items and antique furnishings -- many from the Orient. Native American art from both continents, books and tools for *bonsai* enthusiasts, fine paper and stationery and other delights are featured. It is rare to find a shop with such fresh and unpredictable offerings.

Garden plants, water features, garden furnishings and a large collection of unusual pots and planters are for sale in the garden center along with a selection of *bonsai* for sale ranging in price from charming, tiny saplings undergoing Basic Training to impressive ancient trees collected from far-off places and skillfully replanted in appropriate containers.

Directions: Hwy 3 south to Hwy 16. Elandan Gardens and Gallery, easily recognizable with the huge stone dolmen at the entrance, is located along State Hwy 16 on the south shore of Sinclair Inlet between Port Orchard and Bremerton. (Visitors approaching from Bremerton must pass the gardens and turn around at the legal U-turn just beyond to reach the entrance.)

Information: 360/373-8260, 3050 W State Highway16, Port Orchard (just past mile marker 28,) *elandangardens.com*

Hours: Open Tuesday through Sunday from 10 AM to 5 PM, Closed Mondays and the month of January.

Admission: Admission to the outer garden, garden center and gift shop is free. Admission to the special *bonsai* collection is: senior and general admission, $5.00; Children, $1.00. Special group rates are also available.

Port Orchard City Hall

Port Orchard is the county seat of **Kitsap County**. All the county offices are located together on a hilltop that overlooks the main part of town. A short drive up the hill will take you to a different world full of bureaucratic buildings, lawyers, politicians and people looking for parking spaces.

You'll know you've reached the center of town when you see Port Orchard's new **City Hall**, easily the most noteworthy and prettiest building in town. It has a tall clock tower with chimes that can be heard on the half hour.

A municipal marina lines the waterfront, often berthing boats from as far away as B.C. and Alaska. The marina also features a park which provides a venue for concerts on summer evenings, as well as the annual **Seagull Calling Contest and Festival** each May. It is also the location of the **Fathoms o' Fun** festival including fireworks on July 4.

The main shopping area is nicely connected by the continuous awnings and boardwalk that make for comfortable strolling during our legendary rainy spells.

Port Orchard is a great place to look for antiques. Several antique shops are located downtown on the boardwalk.

An interesting historical note is that from 1910 to 1915 Port Orchard was home to the finest ice cream parlor in the Northwest, the soda fountain at Sponogle's Port Orchard Pharmacy. Advertisements from that time boasted of their "soda fountain genius" and one of the most popular selections was the "buffalo nut" sundae with peanuts and walnuts.

A small foot ferry connects Port Orchard to downtown Bremerton's Washington State Ferry dock, and tour ships offer a cruise around the shipyard.

There is more to Port Orchard than the original downtown area. (Originally the settlement was called "Sidney" and the name persists in the names of some streets and landmarks.)

Several new shopping areas to the south attract customers from Port Orchard's 'burbs and other parts of South Kitsap. A portion of the population commutes to Seattle daily via the Southworth/Vashon ferry.

If you follow the main street to town and make the turn to the south, you will come to Kitsap County's first roundabout (the second being on Bainbridge Island), and just south of it are two nouveau- Victorian buildings of note. The pink one of these "painted ladies" is **Springhouse Dolls & Gifts**, with its **Victorian Tea Room**. The purple one houses a nice bookstore and some offices.

Further south a few miles along Jackson Street is **South Kitsap Community Park**, where you will find a 7½ inch gauge miniature steam-powered train and an enthusiastic group of volunteers who operate and maintain it. With a name that might sound more like a Pacific Northwest clambake, **Kitsap Live Steamers** offers rides from spring through fall over 5,000 feet of track including a trestle and bridge.

Just east beyond the main downtown area, **Beach Drive** begins its winding way along the shore to the northeast. The homes along this road enjoy a fabulous, unobstructed view of Sinclair Inlet and the Olympic Mountains.

Follow the road around the curve to the south to **Manchester State Park**. In the early 1900s it was Artillery Battery Mitchell which together with Fort Ward on Bainbridge guarded Rich Passage, gateway to the naval shipyard at Bremerton, like a pair of Chinese temple dogs.

Today the park has 37 tent and 15 RV sites, as well as picnic grounds, beach access and a group camp area. The skeleton of the old torpedo building is now a picnic shelter, and you can discover other relics of its military days.

Directions:
Hwy 3 south to Hwy 16. Take the turnoff to Hwy 160.

Information:
Port Orchard Chamber of Commerce 360/876-3505, 1014 Bay St Suite 8, *portorchard.com/chamber*

Kitsap Live Steamers, Open April through October, 2nd and 4th Saturdays of each month, 10 am to 4 pm, *kitsaplivesteamers.org*

Springhouse Dolls & Gifts, 360/876-0529, 1130 Bethel Av, *springhousegifts.com*

Manchester State Park, *parks.wa.gov/parks*

Point Robinson Lighthouse

We drove off the ferry at Vashon Island on a sunny autumn morning, not really knowing what to expect or where to go. Inquiring about any tourist attractions, we were told that some people like to visit the **Point Robinson Lighthouse**. We knew there had to be more to it, so we started to explore.

We took a leisurely drive down quiet country roads, stopping at small shops and galleries along the way. It didn't take long for us to realize that the island itself was the attraction we sought — the friendly, casual attitude of the people, the picturesque farms, the changing vistas of water and distant mountains. We were soon completely won over.

The town at **Vashon Center**, little more than a cluster of buildings at an intersection in the middle of the island, has the feel of a Norman Rockwell painting with real rural home-town atmosphere.

Located between two large cities, Seattle and Tacoma, the island is completely dependent on the ferry system to Seattle and the Kitsap Peninsula on the north end, and Tacoma on the south.

With a population of around 10,000 people, Vashon is lightly populated compared to the surrounding urban areas.

But one look at the ferry lines that are an integral part of life discourages many people from moving here (much to the delight of the long-time residents). Vashon Islanders have steadfastly resisted a bridge to the Kitsap Peninsula, and think the ferry does a great job both connecting them to the mainland and limiting growth.

For visitors, it's a fine day trip or overnight stay offering an opportunity to soak up the ambience of a place without traffic lights, condos, fast food or heavy traffic. There are numerous B&Bs, as well as American Youth Hostel accommodations in a tepee or covered wagon.

The community actually consists of two islands, Vashon and Maury, which are connected by a causeway. Several local businesses are well-known regionally or even internationally: Wax Orchards, Seattle's Best Coffee, Island Tofu, and Misty Isle Farms organic beef. K2, manufacturers of skis, bikes and in-line skates, originated here.

Quartermaster Harbor, a bay formed by the two islands, couldn't be a better place to keep a boat, and the roads along the shore offer stunning views, including a fireworks display on July 4.

Like our own Bainbridge Island, Vashon's agriculture was rooted in (ouch – pun!) the strawberry industry. It was on Vashon that the Mukai family developed a freezing method that expanded the strawberry market forever. Kuni Mukai broke the cultural mold by designing the gardens there, a privilege only available to men in her native Japan. Their homestead may be open by appointment - check with the Chamber of Commerce.

The historic **Harrington-Beall Greenhouse Company** was on the forefront of the horticultural industry, cultivating orchids and roses for more than a century, until the operations were relocated to Bogota, Columbia, in 1989. The 23-acre complex was once the largest rose grower in the US. The history of greenhouse technology is reflected in the 59 structures on the premises. Listed with the King County Landmarks and Heritage Commission and the National Trust for Historic Preservation, this site is available for tours if you make arrangements ahead of time. Again, check with the Chamber of Commerce.

Modern-day horticultural needs can be met at several island garden centers and nurseries including **Colvos Nursery** (known for bamboo), **DIG** and the **Topiary Store**.

The cultural center of the community is the **Blue Heron Art Center**, just south of Vashon Center, where a gallery features the works of the many local artists, various classes are offered, and a small theater provides a venue for plays, films and poetry readings.

Island residents celebrate their history with the annual **Strawberry Festival** in early July. Other events including concerts, gallery tours and an annual garden tour are scheduled throughout the year.

Throughout the summer you can visit the **Vashon Winery** and taste their wines and ciders.

In addition to sweeping rural countryside, Vashon has a number of public parks, with several on the water.

Fern Cove Park on the northwest side is a shady old growth dell with a trail to the beach. On the east side of the island, **Lisabeula Park** is *the* destination for scuba divers. You can explore one of Puget Sound's shallowest shipwrecks, as well as check out the abundant underwater life including the Giant Pacific Octopus. Rental gear and instruction are available locally.

If you don't dive, you can rent a kayak at **Jensen Point** and paddle around the island, stopping at waterfront parks along the way.

Another great way to see Vashon is by bike. Bring your own or rent one on the island.

More than 100 species of birds inhabit the island throughout the year. Tramp Harbor, Quartermaster Harbor and the lighthouse are the best places to see marine birds; Wingehaven Park and Fisher Pond are the spots for forest species.

Don't forget to visit the **Point Robinson Lighthouse**, located on Maury Island, 8 a.m. to sunset. Tours may be arranged at 206/432-5055

Directions: Hwy 3 south to Hwy 16, exit onto Hwy 160 to Southworth.

Information:
Vashon-Maury Island Chamber of Commerce 206/463-6217, *vashonchamber.com*
Blue Heron Art Center, 206/463-5131, *vashonalliedarts.org*
Farmer's Market: Sat 9-2 from April to October at the Village Green in Vashon Center.
Vashon Winery, 10317 SW 156th St, 206/567-0055, *vashonwinery.com*
AYH International Hostel, 12119 SW Cove Rd, 206/463-2592, *vashonhostel.com*
Colvos Creek Nursery, 206/749-9508
DIG Floral & Garden, 206/463-5096
The Topiary Store, 206/567-5047, *topiarystore.com*

What's a "gig"? – A small craft, possibly with a sail, carried on a larger ship. US Commander Charles Wilkes' 1841 charting party set out in a gig which was caught in a storm and found shelter in this natural harbor.

Settled by Croatian fisherman in 1867, and later joined by Scandinavians, Gig Harbor became a fishing port and boat-building center. The harbor is still the home port to an active commercial fishing fleet as well as many pleasure craft. One of the local festivals in the annual **Blessing of the Fleet** in May

When **"Galloping Gertie"** (the first Tacoma Narrows Bridge) opened in the summer of 1940 and was dramatically demolished by storms in November of the same year (everyone has seen

that historic film footage of the bridge undulating wildly and disintegrating), the die was cast that engineers would eventually recoup their losses, learn a few things about suspension bridges and, with the completion of the new bridge in 1950, pave the way for Gig Harbor to become a desirable Tacoma suburb.

You can explore the historic waterfront area on foot following a specially-designed brochure available at the Chamber of Commerce. Many of the early 20th century homes were done in classic Craftsman style.

Gig Harbor is a great place to shop! Ringing the harbor are boutiques, galleries, antiques, crafts and book shops and some unusual specialty shops like Harbor Quilt, Contemporary Dolls, the Keeping Room wine shop and gourmet pantry and *two* shops specializing in wild bird watching. And just outside of town along Highway16 is a factory outlet mall.

Gig Harbor is home to a number of artists, and the local **Peninsula Art League** puts on several art shows each year, including the **Summer Art Festival** in July. Several galleries feature works by local artists year-round.

If you drive along the east side of the harbor, you will eventually reach the **Gig Harbor Lighthouse** at the entrance to the bay. As you return to the town center, you can stop at **Finholm View Climb** for a panoramic view of the harbor and mountains in the background. At the head of the bay along a creek is the **Gig Harbor City Park** with playground and picnic areas. A waterfront park in town, **Jerisich Park**, offers docks and moorage, picnic areas and restrooms.

There are several public golfing opportunities nearby and for gardeners, a trip to **Rosedale**

Gardens, the herb gardens at **Foxglove Gardens and Gifts**, and **Peninsula Gardens** are recommended.

A number of restaurants ranging from casual to fine dining are at your disposal, as well as a collection of bed and breakfasts, inns and hotels.

As this is a town with a maritime history and focus, boat rentals of all kinds are naturally available to the visitor, and scuba divers can check out the remains of Galloping Gertie herself.

If you want to explore the more rural areas of this portion of Puget Sound, check out **Fox Island** and the **Key Peninsula** for country roads and water views (good biking opportunities).

You can also opt for the scenic drive to the north past Gig Harbor City Park, taking Crecent Valley Road to Olalla, Colvos Passage and, ultimately, Port Orchard.

Directions: South on Hwy 3 to Hwy 16. Follow signs.

Information:

Gig Harbor Chamber of Commerce, 3302 Harborview Drive, 253/851-6865 *gigharborchamber.com*

Gig Harbor Peninsula Historical Museum, 4218 Harborview Drive, 253/858-6722 *gigharbormuseum.org*, Tues-Sat 10 AM-4 PM, free admission.

Peninsula Art League, 253-858-8920, peninsulaartleague.com

Rosedale Gardens, 7311 Rosedale St, 253/851-7333

Foxglove Gardens & Gifts , 6617 Rosedale St NW, 253/853-4878

Peninsula Gardens, 5503 Wollochet Dr NW 253/851-8115, *peninsulagardens.com*

Gig Harbor Factory Stores, 2709 Jahn Ave. NW; 360/858-7255

MOUNT WALKER

Eastern Lookout over Puget Sound

Dwarfed by its snow-clad neighbors, **Mount Walker** can be recognized by its zigzag road clearly visible from the east. The 2,835-foot summit is easily accessible by automobile. The 4½-mile-long road to the top is gravel, well-maintained and in good condition. Long vehicles like trailers and larger motor homes are discouraged from taking this road because of the sharp turns, but automobiles and mini-vans should have no trouble.

Once on top of the mountain, you will find two viewpoints, one on the east side and one on the west.

The eastern viewpoint looks out over Hood Canal, Puget Sound, Seattle and the Cascade range, south to Mt. St. Helens and Mt. Hood in Oregon, and north to Mt. Baker near the Canadian border. Seattle looks absolutely diminutive nestled among these countless majestic mountains.

As you go from one breathtaking experience to the next, the western viewpoint looks directly into the crags and glaciers of the Olympic Mountains' highest peaks. Looking down on these broad deep valleys brings a sense of awe, intensified by the extreme silence of this spot.

This is the residence of Black Bear, Deer and Elk, and you are fairly liable to see one of these on your visit. Feeding wild animals is a bad idea, they are unpredictable and can be quite dangerous. Even a fluffy, cuddly little critter may have a large over-protective mother grazing nearby. They can best be enjoyed by slowing down and waving at them through a closed window.

Another creature you may encounter is the Mountain Jay -- cute, friendly birds with the curious habit of being hard to get rid of if you make the mistake of feeding them. Anything you leave momentarily unattended is fair game for them, hence their nickname "camp robbers".

The entire top of Mount Walker is densely covered with native Coast Rhododendrons (R. macrophyllum), which happen to be the State

Flower of Washington. During the month of June, when they are in bloom, masses of their delicate pink trusses can be an overwhelming experience. Washingtonians have an affection for Rhodies, and usually most home gardens contain at least one or two species. (For more on Rhodies, visit **Whitney Gardens** in Brinnon -- see Chapter 26)

Alas, camping is not allowed on the mountain, but there are campgrounds nearby for those who want to stay in the vicinity at Falls View Falls Campground. There is a fairly strenuous hiking trail from the road entrance at the bottom of the mountain that leads to the summit. We admit to not having taken it ourselves, but we did meet a group of people who took the trail and arrived at the top about when we did after about 2 hours of hiking. They had looks of pure exhilaration, and reported that indeed their hike had been a wonderful, scenic experience.

Falls View Falls, or **Campground Falls**, while not as dramatic as Rocky Brook Falls (see Chapter 26), is worth the short walk if you are visiting in the rainy season, from October through April.

On the way to Mount Walker, you will pass by the location of the **Olympic Music Festival** featuring the **Philadelphia String Quartet** on weekends in summer. A turn-of-the-century dairy barn has been transformed into a concert hall. When the weather is fine, patrons can also sit out on the lawn.

You will also drive through the tiny village of **Quilcene**, home of the world's largest oyster hatchery and the Whistling Oyster Tavern. The community celebrates with an annual fair and parade in September.

Directions: To reach Mt. Walker, head south on Highway 101 from Quilcene, 5.6 miles. Watch for a sign that says "Mt. Walker Lookout" on the left side of the highway.

Hours: Dawn to dusk.
Information:
Hood Canal Ranger District North, 360/765-2200, *fs.fed.us/r6/olympic/recreation/reports/report_quil.htm*
Quilcene-Brinnon Chamber of Commerce, 360/765-4999, *www.emeraldtowns.com*
Olympic Music Festival, Hwy north of Quilcene, 206/527-8839, *olympicmusicfestival.org*

You walk down a shady green trail along a rushing stream and suddenly find yourself at the base of 120-foot waterfall that doesn't appear on any road map or have a sign to reveal its whereabouts. But we will reveal the way to this secret, enchanted place only if you promise not to tell anyone else.

We like to visit here at the end of winter, when the thawing snows of the mountains cascade off the top of the falls with a dramatic surge of power. We also like to visit in the dry of summer when the water glides down the rocks in a myriad of graceful rivulets, like those seen a

Japanese woodcut print. At other times of the year we like to visit it just because we like to visit it.

On really warm summer days you can often see a bunch of kids from the neighboring area, splashing about in the pools at the base of the falls (even then, it's still very cold snow-melt mountain water).

This is also a place to find the fabled Water Ouzel, or Dipper Bird, a plain-looking grayish bird about the size of a robin but with the strange habit of walking under water, running along the bottom eating dragonfly nymphs. When they emerge from the water, the birds will stand on a rock and do their little up-down dipping dance. Sometimes they will entertain you for hours. You can dip, too, if you roll up your pant-legs and can tolerate the ice-cold water.

Pack a light snack and a thermos full of hot coffee and sit on a large rock and feel the negative ions rejuvenating your being.

The hydroelectric plant is also interesting and small enough in scale to understand. The water is taken out above the falls and comes down the cliff in a 30-inch metal tube to the concrete building that houses the generator. The water goes through the turbines, then passes under the trail and rejoins the fast-running stream. Also watch for the tiny spring, to the left of the trail just past the building, that flows into the creek. You can watch the grains of sand moving slowly in the water like flakes in a snow globe.

Please respect the pristine nature of this magical place. Bring your own drinking water, and pack out any garbage, especially if it isn't yours. There are no restrooms or trash cans.

On your way to Rocky Brook you will see signs to several other falls in the area, but none of them can match the drama of this hidden wonder.

You may choose to continue up the Dosewallips Road 11 miles on a tortuous gravel surface with hair-raising, guardrail-less dropoffs, winding under unstable rocky cliffs. Finally, after climbing a grade so steep your car won't believe it, you will come to the **Dosewallips Falls**, a mighty stair-step cascade tumbling down 200 feet or so over rocks and boulders.

We saw the falls in late summer and can only imagine what it must be like during the snow melt in spring. A rewarding experience awaits the person intrepid enough to make the trip. Don't even think about trying to take an RV. Not for everyone. We advise parking and hiking in from where pavement stops and the gravel road starts.

Back on the main highway, a short distance to the south in the tiny village of Brinnon is the lovely **Whitney Rhododendron Gardens & Nursery**, where you can pick out plants to take or ship home. They offer a large number of varieties, many of which they have bred themselves. If you're not shopping, there is a small fee to wander through the gardens where there is always something in bloom even if it's not rhodie season (April through June).

Brinnon hosts the annual **Shrimpfest** on Memorial Day weekend, celebrating the beginning of Hood Canal shrimp season. It's a hometown affair with crafts, food, belt sander races and other family fun events.

Directions: To find Rocky Brook Falls, take Highway 101 to Brinnon, then once in town, take the Dosewallips Road 3 miles just over a bridge. Park on the left or south side of the road. From there, follow the creek upstream to the falls, a short trek of about 500 feet.

Hours: Perpetual - best to go during daylight.
Whitney Rhododendron Gardens & Nursery, hsy 101, Brinnon, 206/796-441, *whitneygardens.com*

Dalby's Wheel, Union

The southern Hood Canal area is off the beaten path and often missed by the usual tourist crowds. If you were to sail the 40 miles down the length of the Hood Canal, near the south end you would take a hard left , go another 10 miles and ...stop! That's because it isn't really a canal at all, but a major earthquake fault and glacial scour that filled with sea water after the glacier retreated 11,000 years ago. The epicenter of the 1965 Seattle earthquake was just east of the town of Brinnon, in the middle of the canal.

Several state and county parks are located on the water around the Hood Canal, the largest being **Twanoh State Park** between Union and Belfair. Public clamming is allowed at several of the parks during clamming season.

About 12 miles further south from Brinnon on Highway 101 is the turn-off to the **Hamma Hamma Recreation Area** along the Hamma Hamma River. Most of the year it's basically a nice spot to have a picnic or hike a trail in the Olympic wilderness. But when the salmon are spawning in the fall, it is a great place to watch the large numbers of bald eagles feeding on the exhausted and expiring fish. While the dead salmon are a critical part of the forest ecosystem, "Hamma Hamma" is an indigenous term for the nasty smell that accompanies the annual process.

The road to **Lake Cushman** begins in the small town of **Hoodsport**, a pleasant little beach community that is the home of the **Hoodsport Winery**, which produces a fine selection of fruit wines as well as some familiar grape wines. You can stop into the tasting room for samples. Our favorite is the raspberry, with the rhubarb a close second.

Hoodsport is a popular center for SCUBA diving, especially for beginners, as there are no strong currents and the water is exceptionally clear, with visibility to 50 feet in the winter. Several places rent equipment and offer training.

Lake Cushman, a lake surrounded by mountains and formed by the Tacoma Power dam, is a pleasant drive past some small resorts and several retirement "villages". At the far end of the lake, on the road to Staircase, is **Cushman Falls**, which is an impressive sight in the winter and spring, practically splashing onto the road and rushing under it through a culvert to fall another 100 feet. At the end of the summer it almost disappears, becoming a small dribble hidden among the trees.

Another attraction at the very end of the road on the west end of Lake Cushman is **Staircase Rapids,** with a historic stair-step trail originally created by early explorers for mules to traverse the mountainous area. You can walk the easy two- mile loop trail in 1 to 2 hours.

Slightly south of Hoodsport, the related power station stands boldly along Highway101. It is an elegant neo-classical building looking a bit out of place among the Olympic greenery.

Next, you need to make a choice. Highway 101 continues south to Shelton, and Highway 106 branches off to the east along the Great Bend of the canal. We recommend following the bend to the town of Union, and catching Shelton another time as you return from the ocean via Aberdeen and Hoquiam.

In **Union** the picturesque **Dalby water wheel** can be seen right next to the highway. It was built in 1922 by Edwin J. Dalby, whose father settled in the area in the 1890s. For many years it generated electricity for his home and extensive workshop.

The wheel itself is made of steel and stout enough to last these many years. It was formerly part of the cable car mechanism on Seattle's Yesler Hill run, which is yet another layer over another piece of history—the log slide (the original "Skid Road") to Yesler's mill during the era of Seattle's first pioneer settlement.

A group of interested local Union citizens keep the wheel and the small generator building in good operating condition, and the wheel is usually splashing merrily along from late spring to early fall. To find the wheel, look along the side of the highway just about 100 feet west of the Union post office.

Enjoy the ride between Union and Belfair by looking at the waterfront homes—some of the most interesting, unique and innovative we've seen anywhere.

In Belfair you will have the opportunity to visit one of the "best waterfront projects in the world" as recently honored by an international nonprofit group. This is the **Theler Wetlands,** 135 acres of saltwater and freshwater marshes. There is 1/3 mile of "floating" boardwalk extending far out into the marsh, ¼ mile of bridges and about 4 miles of additional nature trails.

One look at the fantastically carved main gate (next to the **Theler Community Center**) and you will know that you are entering a very special place.

The interpretive center run by the Hood Canal Watershed Project has an outdoor sculpture court with garden areas designed and maintained by local Master Gardeners featuring many native plants and habitats, as well as sculpture by notable local artists. Indoor and outdoor interpretive displays will capture the interest of visitors of all ages.

Local school children and youth are very involved in ongoing studies and displays at Theler. A classroom is part of the complex. At the time of writing, work has begun on the assembly of the skeleton of a gray whale that got beached in the area and met an untimely end.

Theler Wetlands is a bird lover's dream. At the interpretive center you can get a list of the more than 40 species that frequent the forest and marshes throughout the year. See how many you can identify during your visit!

Directions: Hwy 101 south to Hwy 106, go east and north until it joins Hwy 3 just south of Belfair.
Information:
Hood Canal Association, *visithoodcanal.com*
Hoodsport Winery, open daily 360/877-9894, *hoodsport.com*
Hood Canal Ranger Station - Hoodsport/Lake Cushman , 150 N Lake Cushman Rd, 360/877-5254
Staircase Ranger Station, 360/877-5569
Union Country Store 360/898-2641
North Mason Visitor Information Center & Mary E. Theler Community Center, Belfair, 360/275-5548, *northmasonchamber.com*
Theler Wetlands, 360/275-0373 open daily during daylight hours, *hctc.com/~hcwater*

28

PORT TOWNSEND

Jefferson County Courthouse, Port Townsend

Port Townsend is in a class by itself. It's a pleasant time-warp back to an era when life was both simpler and fancier. The town has realized the value of its historic brick-and-stone commercial buildings and gingerbread- trimmed Vic-orian "painted ladies", and today it proudly displays its age, to the delight of visitors.

Among its residents you'll find artists, craftsmen, writers, shipwrights and other adventurous and interesting people. Many of the Victorian homes and buildings are on tour for a fee, and a number have become bed & breakfasts. You should definitely stop at the visitor's center near the entrance to town to get a detailed map and a list of events and places of interest.

The highway winding down the bluff to the shipyards and to the main town has got to be one of the most dramatic entrances anywhere, not a whit diminished by the paper mill and its huge, "fragrant" smokestack.

Port Townsend is geographically divided into two parts: **Uptown** and **Downtown**. **Uptown** was originally the location of fine homes, shops and restaurants. Very proper Victorian ladies never went Downtown, along Water Street, where the wharves, taverns and brothels were found.

Today the **Downtown** area is still the more interesting and lively of the two, full of shops, restaurants, galleries and a few rowdy taverns. Antique shops abound. There are several book shops as well as the nationally acclaimed **Elevated Ice Cream** parlor. Allow yourself plenty of time to explore; you'll want to discover every corner of this interesting town.

Captain George Vancouver was the first European to discover the deep, sheltered bay and he named it for some obscure British peer or naval officer, just as he did many other places around Puget Sound. The town continues to be an important harbor and center for the maritime community, with extensive boatyards teeming with shipwrights. Washington State Ferries provides service from Port Townsend to Keystone on **Whidbey Island** several times a day.

The first settlement was in 1851, and by the late 1800s, it was a very prosperous community. Two factors led to its economic downfall: first, the Northern Pacific railroad decided not to go there, and second, Port Townsend lost out to Olympia on its bid to become the state capital. Thus investment capital fled, (the population suddenly dropped from 20,000 to 3,500) causing the town to become frozen in time, and therefore to be preserved historically intact for later generations, much to our advantage today.

In 1895 a military fort, **Fort Worden**, was established along the Strait of Juan de Fuca, with heavy artillery to guard the entrance to Admiralty Inlet and Puget Sound. The fort was decommissioned in 1955 without a shot ever having been fired in anger, became a state park in 1973, and has been totally restored. Former barracks are now a youth hostel, and officers' houses can be rented for special occasions. You can tour the **Commanding Officer's House** for a complete picture of life at the turn of the 20th century.

If the fort looks vaguely familiar to you, it may be because it has been used as a location for a few Hollywood films, most notably *An Officer and A Gentleman.*

Up the hill are trails that lead to the remains of bunkers and gun emplacements and a fine view of the Strait. The road to the **Point Wilson Lighthouse** right along the shore should not be overlooked, offering a scenic vista as well as a **marine science center** at the end of a long pier.

Nearby **Marrowstone Island** is a more rural community with two state parks. **Fort Flagler State Park** was one of three historic forts guarding the entrance to Puget Sound and offers camping and a hostel, the **Marrowstone Point Lighthouse** and **military museum**, plus stunning views of the Strait, Whidbey Island and Port Townsend. The heritage homes there may also be rented. **Mystery Bay State Park** has saltwater mooring and a view of the Olympics.

Port Townsend is host to many festivals and workshops including the **Wooden Boat Festival**, which takes place at the **Wooden Boat Foundation** at the end of Water Street at **Point Hudson**; the **Rhododendron Festival**, which seems to take over the whole town when the rhodies are in bloom; and the zany **Kinetic Sculpture Race** in early October, when eccentric, human-powered, amphibious vehicles dash Downtown, Uptown, through the bay and a bog, attracting a lot of silly people having the time of their lives.

The **Victorian Festival** in March provides a chance to tour many of the historic buildings, homes and bed and breakfasts.

For a year-round sense of yesteryear, visit the **Jefferson County Historical Museum**, including the jail where literary giant Jack London is reputed to have cooled his heels before he continued on his way to the Alaskan gold fields.

The aptly named **Centrum Foundation**, headquartered at Fort Worden, is the center for many more activities than you could attend in one visit, including the Pacific Northwest Ballet, **Festival of American Fiddle Tunes**, **Port Townsend Jazz Festival**, **Country Blues Festival**, and **Marrowstone Music Festival**, to name a few. They take place in the old Army base auditorium, in the remodeled dirigible-hanger theater at the north end of the parade ground, in various barracks buildings, or spill out onto the lawn. You will clearly want to return again and again.

Directions: Hwy 305 to Hwy 3 North to Hwy 101. Follow signs to Beaver Valley Road.

Information:
General Visitor Information: *pt.guide.com*
Port Townsend Chamber of Commerce 888/365-6978, 360/385-2722, *ptchamber.org*
Fort Worden 360/344-4400 *fortworden.org*
Centrum, Fort Worden 360/385-3102, *centrum.org*
Wooden Boat Foundation, 380 Jefferson St, 360/385-3628, *woodenboat.org*
Fairwinds Winery, 19224 Hastings Av, 360/385-3699, *wineryloop.com*
Sorensen Cellars, 234 Otto Rd, 360/379-6416 *Wineryloop.com*
Elevated Ice Cream Company, 627 & 631 Water St, 360/385-1156 *elevatedicecream.com*
Port Townsend Marine Science Center, Fort Worden State Park, 800/566-3932, *ptmsc.org*
Jefferson County Historical Museum, 210 Madison St 360/385-1003, *jchsmuseum.org*

29

SEQUIM

Sequim (pronounced "skwim") has the unique distinction of being the driest spot in Western Washington. This is because our frequent rains usually come from the southwest, and Sequim is located on the northeast side of the Olympic Mountains. The rain is dumped on the mountains before it ever gets to Sequim, causing a "rain shadow" effect. While the wet side of the range gets **12 feet** of rain per year, Sequim gets only 20 inches. This has caused some rather unique results. Sequim is the only area in Western Washington where farmers have always had to irrigate their farms.

Lavender grows very well in this semi-arid climate. Sequimites are determined to make Sequim the lavender capital of the U.S., if not the world. More than 30 growers are currently located there, some featuring more lavender products than you ever knew existed. Visit a few and wander through the fragrant rows. Sequim's ambitious lavender production is actually beginning to make southern France take notice. **Purple Haze Lavender Farm** is one of the best known.

For a lavender extravaganza, come to Sequim during the annual **Lavender Festival** in July.

If you are a gardening enthusiast, you won't want to miss the **Cedarbrook Herb Farm**. The arid climate makes all the other Mediterranean herbs feel at home as well. The oldest herb farm in the state offers many varieties of herb plants for sale as well as dried flowers, potpourris, herb cookbooks, herb vinegars, garlic braids and other items in the gift shop in their historic farmhouse. The **Petals Garden Cafe** in the greenhouse is one of the top restaurants in Sequim.

Not far to the east is the **John Wayne Marina** on Sequim Bay. "The Duke" loved the Pacific Northwest waters and anchored his yacht, *The Wild Goose*, (a remodeled Navy minesweeper, of course) there next to land that he purchased. He donated part of the land to the Port of Port Angeles for a public marina. It's an interesting place to visit, with a restaurant, picnic tables, and plenty of facilities for visiting boaters. We have been told that members of his family still live and/or visit nearby. Tours of Sequim Bay are provided by a local tour boat company.

The **Seven Cedars Casino**, located prominently along the highway just before you get to Sequim, is not only a place to win or lose a few quick bucks and take part at the delicious buffet, but also to enjoy some incredibly well-done Northwest longhouse architecture and Native American art, including totem poles, all done by native artists and craftsmen.

The venture is owned and operated by the S'Kallam tribe, the original inhabitants of the Sequim area. The gift shop located in the casino is more like a fine art gallery, with many beautiful pieces by local Native American artists. The tribe operates another arts center, the **Northwest Native Expressions Gallery**, directly at the head of Sequim Bay.

In 1977, Emmanuel Manis was digging a pond on his 7-acre Sequim farm and discovered two 6-foot-long tusks. He called in paleontologists from around the Northwest and it was determined that the tusks belonged to an 11,000 year old **mastodon**.

Further excavation turned up the rest of the skeleton as well as the remains of other creatures in a prehistoric water hole. One of the mastodon ribs was found to have an arrowhead embedded in it, proving that humans had occupied the area earlier than previously thought.

An interesting display of the bones found and the story of the Manis adventure can be seen at the **Sequim Museum** in town.

Olympic Game Farm was originally begun as a place to house wild animals which had been trained for Disney nature films by owner Lloyd Beebe. Since then, it has provided a retirement home for many Hollywood animal stars, as well as a breeding center for some endangered species.

Railroad Bridge Park runs along the Dungeness River, which rushes headlong (from 7000 feet to sea-level in about 30 miles) to the Strait. The park features an outdoor amphitheater used for events in the summer, trails along the river, the former railroad trestle bridge, now with plank deck for pedestrians and bikes, and the new **Dungeness River Audubon Center**, an interpretive center offering exhibits and birding classes.

Cyclists will also enjoy the **Olympic Discovery Trail**, providing a mostly off-road route from Sequim to Port Angeles. Eventually the trail will extend 100 miles from Port Townsend to the coast near LaPush.

Also on the way to Port Angeles is the road to **Deer Park**. This Olympic National Forest campground is open after the snow melt and offers spectacular views of the mountains and the Strait. The road is paved only part-way and is not for the faint-hearted. Don't try to bring an RV.

Information:
Sequim Visitors Center, Sequim/Dungeness Valley Chamber of Commerce, 1192 E. Washington St 800/737-8462, 360/683-6197, *visitsun.com*
Sequim Lavender Festival, 877/681-3035, *lavenderfestival.com*
Sequim Museum & Arts Center, 175 W Cedar, 360/683-8110, *sequimmuseum.org*
Cedarbrook Herb Farm - 1345 Sequim Ave S, 360/683-7733, *cedarbrookherbfarm.com*
Seven Cedars Casino 270756 Hwy 101, 800/4-LUCKY-7, *7cedarscasino.com*
Purple Haze Lavender Farm 180 Bellbottom Rd 360/683-1714 *purplehazelavender.com*
S'Klallam Northwest Native Expressions Gallery 360/681-4640, daily 10 AM-6 PM *jamestowntribe.org/gallery.htm*
Olympic Game Farm 1423 Ward Rd, 800/778-4295; 360/683-4295, *olygamefarm.com*
Lost Mountain Winery, 3174 Lost Mountain Rd, 360/683-5229, *wineryloop.com*
Olympic Discovery Trail, *olympicdiscoverytrail.com*

The Dungeness Spit is said to be the longest natural sand spit in the United States. It is called a "living" spit, because it continues to grow up to 14 feet each year, according to the U.S. Department of Fish & Wildlife. Its contours are constantly changing due to currents, tides and waves.

Many shipwrecks occurred on the spit before it became obvious that a lighthouse was an absolute necessity. The Straight of Juan de Fuca had many hazards to navigation, including sand spits, reefs and rocks, but none were so hazardous as Dungeness Spit.

The lighthouse, originally built in 1857, is about five miles or so down the spit. Originally, it was 89 feet tall, but was shortened in 1927 to 63 feet, due to damage from vibrations cracking the walls. Seismic activities contributed to the damage, as well as the constant pounding of waves in winter storms.

The original lamp was fired with lard oil, but was replaced in 1880 by a mineral oil lamp and later by an incandescent oil vapor lamp. In 1904

additional living quarters were built, which still remain.

The light was modernized once more with a quartz-iodide light in 1976 and completely automated in 1994. U.S. Lighthouse Society members now staff the facility, giving tours from 9 AM till two hours before sunset to those intrepid enough to make the five mile hike. (If you are interested, inquire about joining the Lighthouse Society and waiting your turn to have a week-long idyllic vacation.)

The entire spit is a wildlife refuge and there are some rules which must be observed: 1) no dogs, beach fires or driftwood collecting, 2) visitors must hike on the seaward side and not on the bay side, which is the nesting area for the many seabirds that live there, and 3) no one but the lighthouse keepers are allowed on the spit after dark.

There are lookout points for the bay side, where you may see loons, widgeons, herons and scoters. On the seaward side you will see cormorants, grebes, murres, and oldsquaws bobbing up and down on the swells.

Camping is not permitted on the spit, but there are 65 campsites in the upland **Dungeness Recreation Area** adjacent to the spit, which are open in summer only. Several helpful volunteer guides are available to answer your questions and provide you with more information. Admission to the refuge is $3 per family and is open year round, from dawn to dusk.

Finding the entrance to the park is a bit tricky -- we recommend stopping at the visitors' center on the highway just as you enter Sequim and getting a free map and directions. They will send you along the most scenic route as well.

Directions: Shorter and less scenic route is Hwy 101 west of Sequim to Kitchen Dick Rd. Turn north and follow signs to Dungeness Recreation Area. Continue through the park to the Refuge parking lot.

Information:

Dungeness Recreation Area 360/683-5847
wa.gov/clallam/parks/dungspit.html

Dungeness National Wildlife Refuge 360/457-8451, *visitsun.com/dungeness.html* Open daily sunrise to sunset

New Dungeness Chapter of the Lighthouse Society of US Lighthouse Society, 360/683-9166
ndlightstation.com

View from Ediz Hook

Port Angeles is the host city for a mountain wonderland on the north slope of the Olympic Peninsula, and a good place to use as a home base, with its restaurants and lodgings. Stop at **Swain's,** the last of the old-time general stores, to pick up hiking and camping equipment at a good price.

Once a S'Klallam fishing village, the harbor was named orginally by Spanish explorers who discovered it in 1791. Port Angeles was the focus of political intrigue in the 1860s when customs inspector Victor Smith decided that he wanted to relocate the custom house, currently in Port Townsend, to Port Angeles. He sailed into Port Townsend's harbor in a warship with its cannons pointed at the city and forced the citizens to surrender the customs book.

Further influence by Smith and his associates caused President Lincoln to declare Port Angeles "Second National City" in 1862. If Washington, D.C., had fallen to the Confederates during the Civil War, Port Angeles, with a population of less than 20 people, would have legally become the nation's capital!

Recently another Port Angeles customs agent made history by opening a car trunk and finding a large supply of bomb-making materials. An Algerian terrorist was then chased across the ferry waiting lines and apprehended, averting a plot to bomb either Seattle's Space Needle during the Millennium Celebration or the Los Angeles Airport at a later date. Perhaps Victor Smith is vindicated for his brazen coup, after all.

The city's waterfront is a center of activity with **The Landing**, a mall of shops and restaurants, a visitors' information center, the **Waterfront Observation Tower**, and the **Fiero Marine Science Center**. Look for the topiary octopus near the parking area. Two local wineries, **Olympic Cellars** and **Camaraderie Winery**, will offer you samples at their tasting rooms.

At the **Chamber of Commerce** on the waterfront you can sign up for a tour of secret Port Angleles. Like Seattle's Pioneer Square, a major effort to raise the level of the city streets took place in 1914, known locally as "sluicing the Hogback". Portions of the underground town are now open to the public.

The **Port Angeles Historical Museum** is currently in transition, with some exhibits available and others awaiting the restoration of the future site. Check with the Chamber.

Ediz Hook, another sand spit reaching into the Strait of Juan de Fuca, is the little sister to Dungeness Spit near Sequim. You can drive along the length of Ediz Hook past the industrial areas out to the Coast Guard station and take a walk in the fresh ocean breeze. A bike trail starting at the downtown waterfront also takes you there.

The outer shore is well-known for the flat, oval-shaped rocks of all sizes worn round and smooth by the surf. This beach is strangely fascinating, with the flat rocks clattering in the ebbing surf, and it feels much more remote than it actually is. Recently local folks have taken to creating sculptural arrangements of the Ediz Hook rocks and driftwood right on the beach. The inner lagoon is a good place to watch seabirds, seals, otters and other creatures, and enjoy a unique view of the city. There is a fireworks display on the Fourth of July.

This is also the port city for the **ferry to Canada**. The *M.V. Coho* provides an exciting day trip to the picturesque, very British capital of British Columbia: Victoria. Most of its attractions are within walking distance of the ferry terminal, so you can avoid the expense of bringing your car. There is even a shuttle bus from the Sequim Chamber of Commerce.

Visit the **Royal BC Museum** for a thorough understanding of the history and culture of the early settlers and the native people. It has one of the finest collections of totem poles and masks.

Nearby are the Aquarium, gardens, conservatories and a miniatures museum. Stroll the main street with its shops featuring British teas, china and woolens and excellent restaurants offering the full range of cultures embraced by the bygone Empire. And, by all means, treat yourself to afternoon tea at the **Empress Hotel**.

Craigdarroch, a genuine Scottish castle and museum, is a longish walk or an easy bus ride from the city center. And a copy of **Anne Hathaway's cottage** (Shakespeare's sweetie) is a short bus ride in the other direction.

Inquire about a tour bus to the world-famous **Butchart Gardens**, north of town. This tour will take up most of your day, but if you are really into gardens, it is a required visit. We are partial to the sunken garden in the old quarry (the original section), the most engaging part of what can sometimes seem to be horticulturally overwhelming.

Directions:
Hwy 101 west from Sequim
Information:
Port Angeles Chamber of Commerce
portangeles.net/
Fiero Marine Life Center, Port Angeles City Pier**,** 360/417-6254
Port Angeles Fine Arts Center, 1203 E Lauridsen Blvd, 360/457-3532 *olympus.net/community/pafac/*
Coho Ferry, Black Ball Transport, Inc. 360/457-4491, in Canada 250/386-2202 *northolympic.com/coho/*
Victoria Express 800/633-1589, 360/452-8088, in Canada 250/361-9144, *victoriaexpress.com/*
Royal BC Museum, Belleville & Douglas St 250/356-7226
Empress Hotel, 721 Government St, *fairmontempress.srwhotels.com*, (250) 384-8111
Craigdarroch Castle, 250/592-5323, *craigdarrochcastle.com*
Butchart Gardens, 866/652-4422 *butchartgardens.com*
Greater Victoria Chamber of Commerce, 250/383-7191, *victoriachamber.ca*, *victoriabcguide.com*
Olympic Cellars, 360/452-0160
Camaraderie Cellars, 360/417-3564

On Ron's first trip to the Pacific Northwest 36 years ago, he hiked the trail to **Hurricane Peak** on a sunny summer evening, turned a corner around a clump of Alpine firs and walked into the path of a stag. They both startled each other, and the deer bounded off across the meadow and disappeared. At that very moment, Ron decided that the Pacific Northwest was the place to live. Ever since then, he revisits that site periodically to recreate that feeling.

The meadows and glacier vistas remind you of the Austrian Alps, as shown in *The Sound of Music*. But before you burst into song like Julie Andrews and go skipping off, trampling the wildflowers, remember -- this is a National Park, and the vegetation is strictly protected for the enjoyment of future generations of visitors.

Hurricane Ridge is probably the most easily accessible high country part of Olympic National Park. There are many trails that enable you to enjoy being close to Nature at its wildest. There are even some paved trails that make it possible for disabled people to have the same experience.

Spring arrives late in the mountains, so the spectacular wildflower season is mid to late summer. Often you will see them poking up through melting snow. If you totally fall in love with the wildflowers, you can find seeds in the gift shop in the lodge to take back to your own garden.

At the end of 17 miles of well-paved road that leads to the top of Hurricane Ridge is the **Hurricane Ridge Lodge**. Situated on the south side of Hurricane Hill at about 5,200 feet, it looks into the Elwah Valley and directly at the Carrie and Blue Glaciers.

The lodge, while not offering overnight accommodations to the public, does contain a restaurant, interpretive center, and downhill and cross-country ski rental service in season. It is one of the few vantage points where you can see the elusive and impressive **Mount Olympus**, the center and tallest mountain of the Olympic range, with its five peaks crowning the summit and glaciers flowing between the peaks.

In the peaks to the north of the road you can often see mountain goats frolicking on the rocks. The parking area is notorious for deer who love to mooch. At first you will be amazed to see them so close and so bold. Later you may be hiding in your car to escape them. Remember, this is a National Park, and feeding them is not only a bad idea but also against the law.

The **Hurricane Hill Trail** provides a 3-mile roundtrip hike to a spectacular 360-degree view. Only 660 feet above the parking lot elevation, it might seem a snap, but most of the gain occurs in the last third of the trail, which is fairly steep with dropoffs. The nearby **Meadow Loop Trail** is still very scenic, only one mile long and completely paved. Both it and the first half mile of the Hurricane Hill Trail are wheelchair accessible.

Near the lodge you can find the 1 ½ lane gravel road that leads to **Obstruction Point**, along the top of the Ridge. The turnoff from the main road feels like the first hill in a roller coaster. In some places along the way, you can look straight down on both sides of the road. (This can be a white-knuckle trip for flat-landers.) We can best describe this as a real mountain road, and scary but safe. Always anticipate another car coming around the next curve, and you won't get into trouble.

The road is 8 miles long, and you can stop and climb the rocky peaks of several mountains along the way. At the end of the road is a parking area from which you can hike into the interior just a

short way until seeing another human being becomes a real event. This is well above the timberline, and you will very likely encounter snow fields, even in August.

In the winter the Hurricane Ridge road is usually plowed clear, except in the worst of winters. Would you like to see a 20-foot snowbank? There's usually one at the edge of the parking lot. Snow commonly gets that deep up here in winter.

The only downhill skiing area in the Olympics, the park has two rope tows and is frequented mainly by locals and lots of kids. There are also miles of trails for cross-country skiing, but there are often snow cornices on the ridge, and you never know when just below you is only air, so always check in at the lodge and follow their safety recommendations. There is a 3-D model of the surrounding area that is a great resource to check over before you go hiking or cross-country skiing.

Directions: Follow signs from downtown Port Angeles
Information:
Olympic National Park Visitor Center, 3002 Mt Angeles Rd & Race St, Port Angeles, 360/565-3130 *olympic.national-park.com*
Hurricane Ridge Visitor Center 360/452-4501
For snow and road conditions 360/565-3131
Bus tours to Hurricane Ridge:
Olympic Bus Lines 800/4457-4492, 360/417-0700, *olympicbuslines.com*
Clallam Transit 800/858-3747, 360/452-4511 *clallamtransit.com*

LAKE CRESCENT & HOT SPRINGS

If you were to do no more than drive past Lake Crescent on Highway 101, you would still be enchanted by its clear blue water, the surrounding mountains and picturesque shoreline. It always reminds us of the road along Loch Lomond in Scotland.

Lake Crescent is 9 miles long, 1 mile wide and 624 feet deep. The elevation at the surface of the lake is 574 feet above sea level.

In the fall, stands of vine maples, plentiful around the lake, turn a brilliant scarlet against the deep green of the firs, hemlocks and spruce. The lake is partially within the boundaries of the Olympic National Park, which has spared it from commercial development. The park has been sensitively planned to keep buildings and facilities from spoiling the natural scenery. In fact, as you drive from the east 1 ½ miles along the lake, you will probably not even notice the **Lake Crescent Lodge**, nestled in the trees and looking out onto the water.

The lodge is a grand old building, in the tradition of national park architecture of the early 20th century. A historic building, it has hosted many famous guests, including Franklin D. Roosevelt when he toured the area to consider the creation of the national park.

You, too, can be a guest in a room at the lodge or in a lakeside cabin with a fireplace. You can also hike to nearby **Marymere Falls**, only one mile from the highway, which is wheelchair accessible to a good viewing point of the falls. The falls, splashing 90 feet from a cleft in the rock, is a magnificent sight set in an old growth forest.

On the other side of the lake, to the northeast and away from the highway, is the more casual and rustic **Log Cabin Resort**, which has regular cabins all with smashing views and all the conveniences, as well as camping cabins with minimal conveniences (bring your own bedding or rent bedding from the management).

We have it on good authority that "Cressie", the Lake Crescent inhabitant ("monster", "creature") has been sighted consistently during the months of April and July feeding in the shallows here. (Never fear – apparently it's a vegetarian!)

On the north and east sides of the lake is the **Spruce Railroad Trail**, a paved-over rail line built in World War I to log spruce trees for aircraft construction. The war ended before it became fully functional. Today what is left is a scenic, flat and easy four-mile trail with outstanding views.

The **Sol Duc Hotsprings** is one of two thermal springs in the Olympic National Park. This unassuming resort has a restaurant, deli, and cabins. Daytrips are encouraged. Take a hike to

Sol Duc Falls and come back to the resort for a hot bath and the services of a masseur.

Sol Duc Hotsprings is located 14 miles into the Olympic Mountains on a delightful road along the Sol Duc River, gradually gaining elevation along the way. The river originates at the Hoh Glacier on Mount Olympus.

The hot water comes to you courtesy of a major fault line which crosses the Olympic range.

The native people tell the story of two warring dragons tossing boulders, dropping moss and lichen scales and shedding dragon tears to create Sol Duc and the more elusive and undeveloped **Olympic Hot Springs**, which may be found by going up the road along the Elwha River and hiking some 2.5 miles into the wilderness.

Directions: **Lake Crescent** – Hwy 101 west of Port Angeles. Sol Duc Hot Springs – Just west of Lake Crescent, turn left off Hwy101 onto the Sol Duc Hot Springs Road, drive 12 miles into the interior.

Sol Duc Falls –from the Hot Springs, drive 11/2 miles to the end of the road and hike another mile to the falls.

Information:
Lake Crescent Lodge 360/928-3211
lakecrescentlodge.com
Log Cabin Resort, 360/928-3325 *logcabinresort.net*
Sol Duc Hot Springs 360/327-3583
northolympic.com/solduc

NEAH BAY AND CAPE FLATTERY

34

Traditional Makah Ocean-going Canoe

The road to Neah Bay begins just west of Port Angeles. Take the turnoff to Highway 112 and proceed northwest. Just before Joyce, a side trip to the north takes you to the **Salt Creek Recreation Area**, an environmental sanctuary featuring 3 miles of rocky beach, tidepools and marine bird life with picnic area, restrooms and trails.

Shortly after crossing the Lyre River (the outlet of Lake Crescent) Highway 112 swings out to the Strait and, except for a small stretch between Pysht (Clallam for "wind from all directions") and Clallam Bay, hugs the shore all the way to Neah Bay. The Strait of Juan de Fuca Highway SR 112 was designated as the newest National Scenic Byway in Washington State on June 15, 2000 at a presentation in Washington D.C.

Clallam Bay and **Sekiu** are tiny towns that provide all the necessities to dedicated sport fishermen seeking halibut and salmon.

Slip Point, near Clallam Bay, has tide pools as well as ancient fossil beds exposed by natural erosion, and is a noted place to dive for abalone and octopus.

A side road continues 20 miles to **Lake Ozette**, where you can hike another 3 miles to the ocean on boardwalk trails. This is the largest natural lake in Washington State. The **Indian Village Nature Trail** takes you to **Cape Alava**, the site of an Indian village that had been in use for thousands of years before it was buried in a mudslide in the 1400s.

Preserved much in the way Pompeii was, the site was exposed by a 1970 winter storm, revealing five flattened longhouses. More than 55,000 artifacts, well-preserved by mud and water, were reclaimed from the site and are on display at the Makah museum.

You can also see 300-year old petroglyphs on the **Wedding Rocks** between Cape Alava and Sand Point. This is a loop trail along the beach as long as the tide is out.

To get to Cape Flattery, go to the village of **Neah Bay**, home of the Makah tribe, and ask for directions. This will also give you an opportunity to meet some interesting people.

Visit the impressive **Makah Cultural & Research Center** (museum) for an introduction to this fascinating area. The Makah were unlike the inland tribes -- they had large seagoing canoes which held many men, and were used for hunting whales, which were central to their culture.

Recently, after a lapse of about 80 years, a whale was taken amid ancient rituals and celebrations. Of course, there were a lot of other people who protested the killing of whales and a continuation of the practice is yet to be decided. This is not the place to wear your "Save the Whales" T-shirt, but it is an opportunity to meet a proud and ancient people and listen to their point of view.

Check out the venerable **Washburn's General Store** and the **Makah Maiden Cafe**. **Native American Adventures** offers insider tours of the museum, local beaches and other sites.

Neah Bay hosts the **Chito Beach Bluegrass Jamboree** in mid-June and **Makah Days** on the weekend closest to August 26, a 3-day festival with powwow dances, fireworks, a parade and salmon feast, canoe races and bone games.

As you continue on your way to **Cape Flattery**, you will pass some interesting and varied landscape, and the road to **Shi Shi Beach**, where you can camp overnight right near the beach. The road ends near the trail to the Cape, which is only a short walk. From here on, the way becomes an enchanting odyssey. If there are such things as nature spirits, this is one of those places where you can intensely feel their presence.

Cape Flattery is the most northwestern point of the lower 48 states. Here the land ends dramatically in huge rocks beautifully sculpted by the constant surf. Some of the land has been carved into bridges and caves. You never know if the ocean might be vibrating just below your feet. The area is a playground for seals, otters, puffins and many other forms of marine wildlife.

Nearby is **Tatoosh Island**, on which stands the lighthouse which marks the entry to the Strait of Juan de Fuca. The lighthouse was built in 1857, making it one of the oldest in the Pacific Northwest. The water between the cape and the island forms a channel through which we have seen gray whales so close that you can see the barnacles on their backs. The best chance of seeing them is during their annual migration in March and April.

Directions: Most Scenic – Hwy 101 west from Port Angeles to Hwy 112 to Neah Bay. Less Scenic – Hwy 101 west from Port Angeles to Hwy 113, Hwy 113 to Hwy 112 and on to Neah Bay

Information:
Salt Creek Recreation Area, Hwy 101 to 112, two roads just before and just after Joyce lead to the recreation area – follow the signs.
The Makah Nation, *makah.com*
Makah Cultural & Research Center, 360/ 645 2711 *makah.com/mcrchome.htm*
Clallam Bay - Sekiu Chamber of Commerce, 360/963-2339 *sekiu.com clallambay.com*
Native American Adventures 360/645-2554

LA PUSH

The village of **La Push** is located on the small Quileute Indian Reservation, totally surrounded by National Park land on the east and by the Pacific Ocean on the west. Its inhabitants are 807 Native Americans, whose language is unrelated to any other tribal language in the area. Like other Native Americans, they are a sovereign nation with their own government and schools. Recently, their ancestral language, Quileute, has been reintroduced and is now taught to the children in the schools.

La Push is located on the mouth of the Bogachiel River where a jetty extending from the river and St James Island form a semi-protected bay. The name "La Push" is a mispronunciation of the French "la bouche", meaning "mouth". The town depends mainly on fishing for its livelihood. Among the commercial fishing boats on the river you can often still see a traditional cedar dugout canoe with an outboard motor perched on the transom.

Ocean Park Resort , a tribal-owned endeavor, parallels the beach for most of the length of the town. Although the atmosphere is casual, the view is spectacular. The units, which include log cabins, hostel-like A-frame cottages, and a couple of two-story motel buildings, are located almost right on the beach, and where else can you be lulled to sleep by the sounds of surf outside your window?

If you're looking for elegance, rent one of the log cabins. But if it's the view you're after, the upstairs units of the more humble motel buildings can't be beat.

If you are a diehard camper, you can reserve a tepee or campsite just south of the resort. Or you can drive to nearby **Mora Campground**, near **Rialto Beach** in the adjacent National Park, with campsites and picnic tables.

Three exciting beach walks originate in or near La Push, named appropriately **First Beach**, **Second Beach** and **Third Beach**.

We think that **Second Beach** is the most rewarding. The way leads down a short trail through an old-growth forest, then opens dramatically to a vista of sea stacks, rocks, tidepools, surf and beach. Many stone formations there have large bowl-like depressions caused by tidal action. These still contain water at low tide and are warmed by the sun. It's like taking a warm bath with an ocean view. These tidal pools are teeming with life. You can gently tickle sea urchins and starfish.

Migrating gray whales pass by in the spring on their annual journey from their birthing area off the coast of Mexico to Arctic waters. Right in town in the bay of **First Beach** is one of their favorite feeding grounds -- they chase smaller fish into the bay on the incoming tide.

When we were there a few years ago in the middle of April, there were more gray whales and pilot whales than we could count, spouting and breaching all across the bay. We even saw three pilot whales cavorting in the surf just scant feet from the beach. If you visit between late March and early May you will almost certainly see whales. The grand show that we witnessed began about two hours after the tide started coming back in.

First Beach extends from town to about two miles to the south to some very interesting tidal caves that are submerged at high tide but accessible at low tide. **Third Beach** is also beautiful, and offers a much longer walk than the other two, but it's minus the tidepools that make Second Beach so interesting.

Don't try to walk around the headlands from one beach to another. They are impassable, and extremely dangerous. Be mindful of the tides -- six hours is a long time to be stranded somewhere. Having a current tide table is a very good idea.

Don't expect fancy restaurants out here. There is a small grocery store in town where you can subsist on snacks or buy groceries that you can prepare in the kitchenettes of most of the units at Ocean Park Resort. Or, if you are too tired from your marathon beach walks to cook a substantial meal, you can drive to **Forks** (page 70), about half an hour away, for an assortment of restaurants.

Off the LaPush road there is a State Park campground at **Mora**, and that road continues to **Rialto Beach**, which has another fantastic view with a wider vista than the beaches at LaPush, but somehow seems spooky to us.

Directions: Hwy 101 west and then south until just before Forks. Turn right (west) on Hwy 110 and follow signs.

Information:
LaPushOcean Park Resort 800/487-1267, *ocean-park.org*
Quileute Tribal Center 360/374-6163

The town of **Forks** is named for the fork in the river where the Bogachiel and Calawah flow into the Quileute River just east of town. Formerly a rugged logging town where loggers stomped around in their cork boots, Forks lost 80% of its economic base in the past 20 years with the decline of the logging industry. (Light-hearted banter about spotted owls does not go over too well around here.) For a town that lost most of the main reason for its existence in one fell swoop, it currently seems to be doing quite well and is looking more prosperous than ever.

The community has recently become a model of 21st century Internet connectivity, bringing broadband to local schools, government and businesses.

To really get in touch with the colorful history of the "West End", as locals call this area, you couldn't do better than visit the **Forks Timber Museum**, just south of the center of town. It features an authentic logging camp and exhibits of pioneer and regional history.

Do you know the difference between a "schoolmarm" and a "grouse ladder" (both types of trees)? Or a "gut robber" and a "donkey puncher" (types of logging camp jobs)? Would you rather ride on a "crummy" or a "speeder"? Find the answers in the little handout *Dictionary of Logging Terms* available at the museum.

The museum was built with pride by the high school carpentry class, with donations of time and exhibit materials from many local volunteers.

One interesting bit of information is that the term "lumberjack" was not generally used on the West Coast. Here the men were known as "loggers".

Adjacent to the museum is the **Forks Loggers Memorial**, gardens, and a forest trail. You can also take a 2 to 3 hour tour on a real logging crew bus visiting mills and logging sites.

At the north end of town in **Tillicum Park** you can see the Rayonier Number 10, a 1930s logging locomotive. This 3-truck Shay, geared steam locomotive was particularly suited to steep logging grades. It was retired from use and donated to the city in 1959. Efforts are now being made to give it better protection from the elements.

An inspired arts community turned a 1925 building in downtown Forks into the **Rainforest Arts Center**, which sponsors events, shows and performances. The annual **Rainfest** in April features arts, music, dance and other performances.

To visit local artists and craftsmen in their studios, galleries and shops, inquire at the Chamber of Commerce for the **Olympic West Arttrek** guide and map.

Forks has a real hometown **Old Fashioned Fourth of July** celebration, complete with fireworks.

Forks, or nearby La Push, is a good place to make your home base for a thorough exploration of the West End. A number of motels, bed and breakfasts, and inns provide lodging. The Forks Chamber of Commerce offers a brochure describing several interesting day trips with Forks as the hub.

Information:
Forks Chamber of Commerce, 800/443-6757, 360/374-2531, *forkswa.com*
Forks Timber Museum, 360/374-6807, 10 to 4 daily
Olympic West Arttrek 800/44FORKS
northolympic.com/arttrek

World Champion Western Red Cedar

The Hoh

Many people believe that they have to drive up the Hoh Valley to see the rainforest. Actually, once you get out to Neah Bay, or turn south to Forks and La Push, it's *all* rainforest -- almost all the way to Aberdeen and Hoquiam.

The Olympic Mountain range traps the wet weather from the ocean, and most of it falls right there on the western side, with an average of **12 feet per year**, much of which stays in the high canopy and never reaches the ground.

People have tried to describe the many shades of green, the fog that surrounds you like a blanket, the mosses growing on absolutely everything, the scent of damp evergreens, the tremendous variety of plant life covering every bit of ground, and epiphytes (aerial plants) taking up the vertical space as well. The vegetation of this cold jungle is among the fastest-renewing in the

world. And it really needs to be experienced first-hand.

Some of the largest trees in Washington State and the nation are located here. Some are native species; others, like the Sitka spruce and Alaskan cedar, are immigrants whose sizes reach well beyond what is possible in their native land.

Other creatures which relish these conditions include the native banana slug and many types of mushrooms, especially in autumn. Do not be tempted — by the mushrooms, not the slugs! — unless you *really* know what you are doing.

The trip up the **valley of the Hoh** follows the river for 12 miles or so to a ranger station and visitor center. Three loop trails await you. The shortest is the **Mini-Trail**, a quarter-mile loop which is wheelchair accessible. The **Hall of Moss Trail** is ¾ mile long. The **Spruce Trail** runs for 1 ¼ miles.

The Hoh River area was also the home the legendary German settler John Huelsdonk, known as as the **"Iron Man of the Hoh"**. The feats of almost superhuman strength credited to this rugged homesteader, hunter and government guide contributed the factual basis to stories of the mythical Paul Bunyon. His descendants operate a hostel-like B&B on their organic farm in the area.

Did you know ? — most Western Washington grocery stores and hardware stores carry inexpensive, light-weight plastic rain ponchos. If you're planning to visit the rainforest, don't be surprised if it is raining!!

Ruby Beach

Very little of Olympic National Park actually runs along the Pacific Ocean. As Highway 101 goes south from Forks passing Bogachiel State

Park and turning west to the ocean, **Ruby Beach** is the beginning of a short stretch of waterfront national park land.

A picturesque beach almost a mile long, Ruby Beach offers sea stacks and tide pools. The "rubies" are actually tiny garnet pebbles and sand, giving the beach its pinkish hue.

The Numbered Beaches

Maybe it was a bureaucratic government thing, but the spectacularly scenic beaches along this 11-mile shoreline have numbers, not names. All of these beaches have a great view of Destruction Island, with its lighthouse. They begin with 6 at the north end and 1 at the south, and you might notice that for some reason there is no number 5.

Watch for a sign that says "Big Tree" and a small road to the east off the highway. A very short drive and short walk will bring you to a massive **ancient cedar tree**.

Kalaloch

Just down the road, to the south between Beaches 3 and 2, is **Kalaloch Lodge**, one of a few private businesses operating in the national park, a hotel and restaurant combined with a collection of beach cottages. Perched on what Western Washington realtors would call "high-bank waterfront", the ocean waves crash in the small bay down below. With a long history dating back to the 1920s, it's a great place to stay in any season, and an opportunity to eat breakfast, lunch or dinner in a spectacular setting.

A little further south, the tiny village of **Queets** boasts the **world's largest Douglas fir tree** – 220 feet tall and 45 feet in circumference.

Lake Quinault

Lake Quinault is an alpine lake which from the west along Highway 104 appears rather stark and open, belying the true rainforest nature of the area.

Lake Quinault offers two distinct experiences — the north shore and the south shore. And there is a connecting road at the east end which ties them together, making a great 30-mile bike trip.

The **North Shore Road**, on the sunny side of the lake, takes you to the **Lake Quinault Resort**, begun in the early 1950s and recently restored and refurbished.

The **South Shore Road** passes the **Lake Quinault Lodge**, built in 1926 and visited by FDR when he was considering the creation of the Olympic National Park.

Further along the road, the **Rain Forest Resort** is the location of the **world's largest spruce tree** and fourth-largest tree in the nation (circumference 55 ft., 7 in., diameter 17 ft., 8 in. and 191 ft. tall for a total of 922 AFA points).

At the end of the South Shore Road is the trailhead to the **Enchanted Valley**. A 2.5 mile hike leads to the **Pony Bridge,** a photogenic spot spanning a deep canyon. For overnight hikers, the trail continues, passing many waterfalls and other magical scenery, through the Olympics to the Dosewallips Valley. Unfortunately, at the time of this writing, this trail was out of service due to mudslides. Check with the Quinault Ranger District Office for the current status of the trail.

Directions: 35 miles south of Forks on Hwy 101.
Information:
Hoh Rainforest Visitors Center 360/374-6925
Kalaloch Lodge, 15751 Hwy 101, Forks, WA 98331, 866/525-2562, *visitkalaloch.com*
Kalaloch Visitor Center, 360/962-2283
Quinault Ranger District Office,360/ 288-2525

The North Beach

If the ocean is drawing you like a magnet and you can't seem to get enough of it, head for the group of resort towns collectively known as **"The North Beach"**.

The economic foundation of these coastal villages, in addition to timber processing, was a once-massive clam canning industry. A monumental storm in the 1920s seriously rearranged the shoreland for miles and destroyed most of the cannery buildings and a 285-room hotel.

Today, these communities have a year-round population supported by local shake mills, commercial clamming, and a large influx of tourists in the summer months.

There are many lodging opportunities, from tiny 1940s motel cabins to upscale resorts, and a few B&Bs. RV parks and campsites abound. Food can be found in numerous cafes and restaurants, and grocery stores for do-it-yourselfers. Each community hosts a festival during the summer months, from sandcastle building to kite flying.

But the main attraction is definitely the ocean itself. There are no sea stacks here—just the vast expanse of ocean and uninterrupted beaches which stretch for more than 22 miles. This is one place where you will *definitely* need a local tide table. You can walk, sunbathe, rent a horse, build a sandcastle, splash around in the surf, and prowl around looking for treasures just recently swept in. Coals from Newcastle are still washing up from a shipwreck on the Copalis Rocks, and a few years ago a shipping container went overboard and provided free ice hockey equipment on every new tide.

If you don't want to walk, you can *drive*—12 miles of beaches are open to vehicles year round, and another 8 ½ are open in summer. Make sure you get a local tide table.

Of course you will need to dodge the beachcombers, horseback riders, clam diggers and beach logs. Maximum speed is 25 MPH. Care is advised in crossing streams which empty into the sea, and you are warned not to drive in the surf or on dry sand. There are basically no towing services, and stuck cars have been known to sink out of sight. Try explaining *that* to your insurance company!

Splashing in the shallows can be fun, but real swimming can be dangerous because of undertows and rip tides. Ask the locals. Surfing is possible at **Ocean City** and **Pacific Beach State Parks.**

You can even learn how to dig razor clams if you come during clamming season, usually starting in April. Check with WA State Fish & Wildlife 360/249-4628 for information on dates and necessary license fees.

Moclips, once the home of the 285-room hotel, is the smallest and sleepiest of the four towns.

The next two as you proceed south on Highway 109, **Pacific Beach** and **Copalis Beach**, are progressively larger, and **Ocean City,** the furthest south of the four, is the largest. It is the location of the **Washington Coast Chamber of**

Commerce, which serves them all, and the **Dorothy Andersen Cabin and Museum**.

Dorothy Andersen was a Norwegian immigrant who built herself a log cabin in 1926. She had a little help from a part-time handyman, but dragged all the lumber up from the beach herself in a wheelbarrow and trimmed the boards with her Norwegian yak knife. The beadboard ceiling was salvaged from a shipwreck. She went on to build eight more cabins and operated "Dorothy's Tourist Harbor" for many years.

Ocean Shores

This place is unlike anywhere else on the Peninsula. You'll feel like you stepped into the Star Trek transporter and were suddenly plunked down somewhere in Florida.

Once a 6,000 acre cattle ranch, this 6-mile long peninsula was purchased in 1960 by investors who wanted to turn it into a major convention and tourism center. A freshwater lake and 23 miles of canals were dug (for "waterfront" homes) and stocked with sport fish. The requisite golf course and even a small airport were built. Their plans didn't pan out, probably because of the distance to the Puget Sound urban areas (the four-lane freeway to Olympia wasn't finished until the mid 1980s).

Over time Ocean Shores has become a sort of suburb for Hoquiam-Aberdeen and is also a popular summer vacation destination. There are resort and convention hotels, motels and vacation condos, restaurants, gift shops, a multiplex cinema and all sorts of diversions. It offers many opportunities to entertain bored children. If you're looking for a convention location that offers salt air and a change of pace, this could be it -- if you can maintain the same cold-blooded attitude the locals have toward possible tsunamis. This is not the beach for walks in quiet solitude, although the **North Jetty** at the

southwestern tip of the peninsula provides a romantic spot to watch the sunset. The beach at Ocean Shores bustles with activity — rented mopeds, horses, kites, dune buggies and the like. A host of festivals attract visitors throughout the year, including the **Harley Owners Group Sun & Surf Run** in late July. If the usual mopeds and hot rods haven't generated enough ruckus, and you're ready for a lite version of Sturgis, South Dakota, this one's for you.

One of the most interesting and most overlooked areas of Ocean Shores is the **marina and Damon Point** at the southern tip, known for surfing and windsurfing. The nearby **Oyhut Wildlife Recreation Area** provides a marshy habitat for more than 200 species of birds, including nesting sites for the endangered snowy plover and semipalmated plover.

All-Weather Tourism

Don't overlook the possibility of visiting the ocean in winter. You'll have the place pretty much to yourself, and you can enjoy the peace and quiet of the beach minus the dune buggies and mopeds of summer. In brisk weather the ocean is wild—beach walks can be exhilarating if you dress appropriately, and a 40-knot gale makes cuddling up in front of a fire with a good novel even more appealing.

Directions: Just south of Lake Quinault and Neilton, a side road, the Moclips "highway" branches off from Highway 101. It is paved for about 15 miles, with a 5-mile stretch of gravel road in good condition.

Information:
Washington Coast Chamber of Commerce, 2616A SR 109, Ocean City, WA, 800/286-4552, 360-289-4552, *washingtoncoastchamber*.org
Ocean Shores Chamber of Commerce, 800/762-3224, 360/289-2451, *oceanshores.org*
Tide Tables Online *tidesonline.nos.noaa.gov*

Hoquiam's Castle

Located on the Washington State coast's only deepwater port, **Grays Harbor**, the twin cities of **Aberdeen** and **Hoquiam** were natural outlets for the 19th century timber industry. By 1910, more than 30 timber mills were located here.

Aberdeen was obviously named for the city in Scotland (whose name means "meeting of two rivers"), and "ho-qui-umpts" was the name given by Native Americans to the driftwood- intensive mouth of the Hoquiam River. It meant "hungry for wood", rather prophetic and ironic at the same time.

Once they were clearly distinct towns, but over time development caused them to blend into each other, and a visitor is hard pressed to notice where the city limits lie between them. Aberdeen's population is around 17,000, and Hoquiam's is about half that size.

The abundance of lumber made Grays Harbor an important ship-building center. Furniture, woodworking and plywood factories were built. Pulp and paper mills also abounded, and the resulting air quality was such that the Grays

Harbor College teams were called "The Chokers."

Just inside the north side of Grays Harbor and west of the cities, with air kept clean by prevailing winds, is the 500-acre **Grays Harbor National Wildlife Refuge** at **Bowerman Basin.** The mudflats teeming with little crustaceans make this spot one of four major staging areas in North America for a million or so shorebirds in April and May. Some birds come from as far away as Argentina. One to two hours before and after high tide is when the action is.

Birders will not be disappointed if they come at other times of year as well, as many marine birds, shorebirds and predators are found in the area. This refuge is home to many of the same endangered species that are found at Damon Point at Ocean Shores. The path is often muddy, so be prepared.

Hoquiam is probably best know for **Hoquiam's Castle**, one of two mansions built next to each other by the Lytle brothers. High on a bluff overlooking the town and the harbor, they gave this lumber family a physical and psychological advantage over the other citizens. Hoquiam's Castle (1897) was a museum for many years, and is now a bed and breakfast.

Polson Park, next to the river, was once the estate of another lumber baron, Alex Polson, who owned what was for its time the largest logging company in the world. The 1924 mansion now open to the public belonged to his son. His own mansion was destroyed by his wife after his death (apparently she could not abide the idea of anyone else ever living there), and that area now features a rose garden and steam train.

On the second floor of the mansion is an HO scale model railroad depicting historical Hoquiam in the heyday of the lumber industry.

The **Aberdeen Museum of History** offers much information about the local timber industry, as well as exhibits of early firefighting equipment.

Probably the most famous resident of Aberdeen-Hoquiam is the ***Lady Washington***, a full-size replica of the brigantine sailing ship which was in 1788 the first American vessel to explore Northwest waters, captained by Robert Gray, discoverer of the Columbia River. The new *Lady* was finished in 1989 and sports two masts, 12 sails, 4,400 square feet of canvas and more than 6 *miles* of rigging.

When she is at port, you can find her at **Grays Harbor Historical Seaport** on the Wishkah River.

Although her image is the symbol of the twin cities, she is most often somewhere else -- Puget Sound, Port Angeles, Port Townsend -- doing what she does best: sailing. The *Lady Washington* is available for short trips lasting a couple of hours as well as longer voyages, sometimes ocean-going. If you get a chance to take a trip, do it! Long or short trip, everybody on board gets a chance to help, hauling the lines or the anchor, singing along with the shanty-man. We played bagpipes and drums as our contribution.

The twin cities celebrate July 4th with an all day family festival including fireworks over the Chehalis River.

September is the time to visit Hoquiam for the logging festival, **Logger's Playday**. For more than 35 years, national and international competitors have gathered for log rolling, tree topping, ax throwing and other traditional events.

Directions:

Information:

Grays Harbor Chamber of Commerce and Visitors Center, 506 Duffy St, Aberdeen 360/532-1924, *tourismgraysharbor.com*

Grays Harbor Historical Seaport 800/200-LADY, *ladywashington.org*

Arnold Polson Park and Aberdeen Museum of History, 1611 Riverside Ave, Hoquiam, 360/533-5862

Grays Harbor National Wildlife Refuge 360/532-6237, *graysharbor.fws.gov/*

Westport Historical Museum

Westport

A half-hour drive from Aberdeen, **Westport** guards the southern entrance to Grays Harbor, across the bay from Ocean Shores. In summer, a passenger ferry plies between the two locations, and whales are often seen along the route.

Westport has plenty of amenities and interests for visitors, but it remains an authentic, mainly un-touristed community. Surf shops rent wet suits and offer instruction. Whale-watching boats depart frequently during the migration seasons. Kite shops offer an imaginative variety of designs.

In the past this town proclaimed itself "Salmon Capital of the World", but that was before the short seasons were imposed due to declining runs.

Westport is still a busy center for commercial and sport fishing. The fishing charters don't provide meals, but the local restaurants have evolved extra-early breakfast hours for fisherfolk, and can also provide a packed lunch.

Local attractions and shops most interesting to visitors are clustered around the harbor. These include the **Shell Museum**, **Westport Aquarium**, a kite shop, book shop, antique shops, gift shops and several restaurants.

The **Westport Historical Maritime Museum**, located at the harbor in a former 1939 Coast Guard Station with regulation Nantucket architecture of the period, will make you think you are on the set of a remake of *Moby Dick*, instead of the shores of the Far West. The museum takes you through the sea-faring history of the area, including the rescues managed from this station. One exhibit is the original Fresnel lens from the Destruction Island Lighthouse.

Whale skeletons are on display in a covered exhibit outside that can be seen at any time of day.

The museum is also the start of a seven-mile **Maritime History Trail** which leads the visitor around the town to historic locations including the **Grays Harbor (Westport) Lighthouse**.

Now part of the **Westport Light State Park**, the lighthouse stands several hundred yards inland from the shore. Over the past hundred years or so, the sand has built up in front of it and is now the site of a two-mile paved **Dune Interpretive Trail.** The lighthouse is generally closed to the public, but special tours may be arranged through the museum.

Westport celebrates Independence Day, like many other cities on the water, with the **Booming Bay Fireworks Display**.

Grayland

South of Westport on Highway 101 is the town of Grayland, famous for its cranberry industry. Nicknamed "The Cranberry Coast", It was settled by Finns who converted the peat bogs into cranberry bogs. *Ocean Spray*® really does get ocean spray around here. There are some great ocean beach parks along the road, and a **cranberry museum** in Grayland, featuring the creativity of Julius Furford, inventor of the cranberry harvesting machine. The town celebrates the past and the present at the annual **Cranberry Harvest Festival** in October.

Several ocean-front state parks offer rewarding vistas, **Westhaven** and **Westport Light State Park** in Westport, and **Twin Harbors**, with its **Shifting Sands Nature Trail** through the dunes, and **Grayland Beach State Park**.

If you go south all the way to **North Cove**, you will be at the northern entrance to **Willapa Bay**, the pristine estuary famed for bird life and oysters, where 7.5 millions of gallons of water per second cross the bar with every tide.

Directions: From Aberdeen take Hwy 105 south and west to Westport. Continue south on 105 to Grayland.

Information:

Westport Historical Maritime Museum, 2201 Westhaven Dr, 360/268-0078, 10-4 daily, Memorial Day through Labor Day

Westport Aquarium, 321 E Harbor, 360/268-0471

Westport-Hoqiuam Passenger Ferry, 360/268-0047

Westport-Grayland Chamber of Commerce, 2985 S Montesano St, 800/345-6223, 360/268-9422, *westportgrayland-chamber.org*

Furford Cranberry Museum, 2395 St Hwy 105, 360/267-3303

Grayland Pacific Center of the Arts & Crafts, 360/267-1351

Twin Harbors State Park, 3 miles south of Westport on Hwy 105, 360/902-8844

Grayland Beach State Park, 5 miles south of Westport and 2 miles south of Grayland on Hwy 105, 360/902-8844

Sooner or later it is time to head back to Seattle, Tacoma, Olympia, or Sea-Tac Airport, and ultimately, home.

The final leg of the Olympic loop, while perhaps not as dramatic as the coastal portion, still holds some secrets and surprises.

US Highway 12 leaves Aberdeen heading east and becomes a freeway (State Highway 8) at Montesano.

Wynoochee Falls is on the Wynoochee River north of the dam at Wynoochee Lake. You can look for a second, unnamed falls on the way. The river below the dam is famous for fly fishing and whitewater kayaking. This pristine area has relatively few visitors. The road may be closed in winter.

Lake Sylvia, a small state park at Montesano, offers a 2-mile hike and camp sites with a water view.

Friends Landing is a nature reserve along a half mile of the Chehalis River which has a been designed as a haven for the disabled, with a handicapped access loop trail, RV sites, boat ramp and other features.

You will notice the non-nuclear cooling towers at **Satsop**, a never-completed nuclear reactor (one of the towers was flooded and used in the filming of *The Abyss*). The site is now a business and technology park. Here you can choose to continue straight on to Olympia, or loop back to Kitsap County.

Elma

The exit for **Elma** is the deciding point. This town of 3000+ was once known for its annual Slug Festival, and later for other festivals complete with air show fly-bys. One year this involved teddy bears parachuting earthwards. Another year it was flour bombs. Now the current festival is called **Outlaw Days** and revolves around stock car races at the Grays Harbor County track.

Elma is best known now for the more than 20 colorful murals by local artists depicting life in the early days of the logging industry. The majority have been painted by James Abbott.

Follow Highway 108 east of town through McLeary to 101 and continue north to Shelton.

Shelton

Shelton, the Mason County seat, is the Christmas-tree-growing capital of the Pacific Northwest. Nicknamed "Christmas Town USA", trees from Shelton have been exported as far away as the Panama Canal Zone, as recounted on a "Christmas on the Isthmus" web site that we found.

Located on a quiet backwater of Puget Sound, Shelton was prime location for oyster farming and logging as far back as 1878 However, pollutants from pulp mills and sawmills contaminated the bays, which have only now recovered 40 years after the discontinuation of the polluting activities. The oyster industry has made a comeback in recent years.

Both historic legacies are celebrated annually, with the **Goldsborough Creek Run & Forest Festival** in early June featuring logging competitions, and **Oysterfest**, the West Coast Oyster Shucking Championship and Washington State Seafood Festival, in early October, a month with an "R". (Oysters are seasonal, hence the old saying ''Never eat oysters in a month without an 'R' in it.'') There are two championship divisions, one for speed and one for half-shell.

Oysterfest offers free entertainment, a seafood cookoff, wine and beer tasting by local wineries and microbreweries, and food vendors who must each offer unique dishes amongst themselves.

The railroad made it to Shelton and featured largely in the logging industry there. Two **old steam locomotives** remain: "The Tollie", Simpson's Logging #7, nicely restored in front of the Post Office, and an 0-4-2T (which has received less attention) in the park in the center of town. This park also features concerts in the summer months.

The **Shelton-Mason County Chamber of Commerce** completes the railway theme in a caboose not far from the post office.

One of the lesser-known attractions around Shelton (which we discovered via an Internet search) is **Arcadia**, a "clothing-optional resort" which promotes itself as a "romantic nudist getaway" on the shores of Puget Sound.

Also somewhere in the Shelton area there is a new commercial plantation for *wasabi*, the green Japanese "horseradish" condiment root which prefers to grow in cold mountain streams.

Directions:

From Aberdeen/Hoquiam: Hwy 12 east from Aberdeen, which becomes freeway (Hwy 8). Exit at Elma and take Hwy 108 through McCleary north to Hwy 101. Continue north to Shelton.

From Bremerton: Hwy 3 south through Gorst, follow signs for Belfair and Shelton.

Wynoochee Falls: Hwy 12 east from Aberdeen to Devonshire Rd, just before Montesano; north to Wynoochee Valley Rd #22 to Forest Service Rd 2270. Go 6 miles and stay right at fork, look for unnamed falls after 1 more mile. Continue north to old campground and walk short trail to falls.

Information:

Lake Sylvia State Park, Montesano (follow signs) 360/249-3621

Friends Landing - 8 mi. East of Aberdeen on Hwy 12 to Aldergrove Rd. Continue south 3 mi. Camping reservations for disabled visitors (360) 249-5117

Elma Chamber of Commerce, 117 N Third St, PO Box 798, 360/482-3055 *elmachamber.org*

Shelton/Mason County Chamber of Commerce, 221 W Railroad Avenue, Suite 5 & 6, 800/576-2021 or 360/ 426-2021, *sheltonchamber.org*

Arcadia, 360/426-7116, *home.sprynet.com/~arcadia*

Appendixes

EVENTS BY MONTH

January

North Beach	Come Have a Ball on the North Beach
Ocean Shores	Sunlover's Indoor Beach Bash
Ocean Shores	Write on the Beach

February

Aberdeen	Rain or Shine Jazz Festival
Bainbridge Island	Chilly Hilly Bike Ride
North Beach	Come Have a Ball on the North Beach
Port Townsend	Chamber Music Festival
Poulsbo	Kitsap Quilters Show
Quilcene/Brinnon	Salmon Derby

March

Grayland	Annual Driftwood Show
North Beach	Come Have a Ball on the North Beach
Port Townsend	Victorian Festival
Port Townsend	Kitemakers' Conference
Port Townsend	Port Townsend Playwrights' Festival

April

Bainbridge Island	Bainbridge Home Tour
Forks	Rain Festival
Hoodsport	Hood Canal Oyster Bite
Hoquiam	Grays Harbor Shorebird Festival
North Beach	State Route 109 Garage Sale

Ocean Shores	Photography & Fine Arts Show
Port Townsend	Port to Port Regatta
Quilcene/Brinnon	Heritage Days
Suquamish	Native American Art Fair
Vashon Island	Spring Fling
Westport	World Class Crab Races & Crab Feed

May

Bainbridge Island	Scotch Broom Festival
Port Angeles	Juan de Fuca Festival
Port Orchard	Seagull Calling Festival
Port Townsend	Rhododendron Festival
Poulsbo	Viking Fest
Quilcene/Brinnon	ShrimpFest
Sequim	Irrigation Festival
Westport	Annual Blessing of the Fleet

June

Bainbridge Island	Rotary Rummage Sale & Auction
Bainbridge Island	Island Days
Belfair	Belfair Summerfest
Bremerton	Concerts in the Park
Gig Harbor	Blessing of the Fleet
Gig Harbor	Maritime Gig Festival
Ocean Shores	International Kite Challenge
Ocean Shores	Northwest Sand Sculpture Open
Ocean Shores	Sand & Sawdust Festival
Port Gamble	Medieval Faire
Port Orchard	Fathoms o' Fun
Port Orchard	South Kitsap Garden Tour

Port Townsend Tour	Jefferson County Secret Garden
Poulsbo	Skandia Midsommerfest
Quilcene/Brinnon	Olympic Music Festival
Sequim	Jazz Festival
Shelton	Mason County Forest Festival

July

Aberdeen	Splash Festival
Bainbridge Island	Grand Old Fourth
Bainbridge Island	Bainbridge In Bloom Garden Tour
Bremerton	Concerts in the Park
Clallam Bay/Sekiu	Clallam Bay/Sekiu Fun Days
Forks	Fourth of July/Fireworks
Grayland	Windrider Kite Festival
Hoodsport	Celebrate Hoodsport 4th of July
Kingston	Fourth of July
Lake Quinault	Lake Quinault Bike Ride
Ocean Shores	Sun & Surf Run - H.O.G.S.
Port Angeles	Fourth of July/Fireworks
Port Gamble	North Kitsap Arts & Crafts Show
Port Hadlock	Port Hadlock Days
Port Orchard	Fathoms o' Fun/Fireworks July 4
Port Townsend	Festival of American Fiddle Tunes
Port Townsend	Jazz Port Townsend
Poulsbo	Fireworks on the Fjord
Suquamish	Fireworks on the Slab
Sequim	Lavender Festival
Shelton	Mason County Fair
Silverdale	Whaling Days
Vashon Island	Fourth of July/Fireworks
Vashon Island	Strawberry Festival
Westport	Booming Bay Fireworks Display

| Westport | Elk River Challenge |
| Westport Classic | Northwest Longboard Surfing |

August

Bainbridge Island	Outdoor Music Festival
Bainbridge Island	Summer Studio Tour
Belfair	Taste of Hood Canal
Bremerton	Kitsap Fair & Rodeo
Bremerton	Concerts in the Park
Neah Bay	Makah Days
Olalla	Summer Bluegrass Festival
Ocean City	North Coast Sky Painters Fun Fly
Port Angeles	Clallam County Fair
Port Orchard Race	Festival by the Bay & Great Ball
Port Townsend	Country Blues Festival
Port Townsend	Jefferson County Fair
Poulsbo	Arts by the Bay
Suquamish	Chief Seattle Days
Westport	Annual Seafood Festival
Westport Carving	International Nautical Chainsaw
Westport	Brady's Annual Oyster Feed
Westport	Westport Art Festival

September

Bremerton	Blackberry Festival
Elma	Grays Harbor County Fair
Grayland	30 Miles of Junque Garage Sale
Hoodsport	Hoodsport SCUBA Festival
Hoquiam	Loggers Play Day
Kingston	Bluegrass Festival
Pacific Beach	Sandcastle Contest
Pacific Beach	Up Your Wind Kite Festival

Port Angeles	Strait Bluegrass Festival	Gig Harbor	Winterfest
Port Ludlow	Port Ludlow Days	Hoodsport	Annual Holiday Festival & Bazaar
Port Orchard	Mosquito Fleet Maritime Festival	Ocean Shores	Dixieland Jazz Festival
Port Townsend	Wooden Boat Festival	Poulsbo	Yule Fest
Port Townsend	Quilting By the Sound	Bainbridge Island	Harvest Fair
Poulsbo	Septemberfest	**December**	
Poulsbo	Renaissance Nights	Bainbridge Island	Mochi Tsuke
Quilcene/Brinnon	Quilcene Fair & Parade	Port Gamble	Country Christmas
Sequim	Dungeness River Festival	Silverdale	Christmas Tree Lighting
Westport	30 Miles of Junque Garage Sale	Vashon Island	Holiday Open House

October

Forks	Heritage Days
Grayland	Cranberry Harvest Festival
Port Townsend	Kinetic Sculpture Race
Poulsbo	Annual Lutefisk Dinner
Shelton	Oysterfest

November

Bainbridge Island	Studio Tour/Christmas in the Country

EVENTS BY CITY

Aberdeen

Rain or Shine Jazz Festival	February
Splash Festival	July

Bainbridge Island

Chilly Hilly Bike Ride	February
Bainbridge Home Tour	April/May
Scotch Broom Festival	May
Rotary Rummage Sale & Auction	June
Island Days	June
Grand Old Fourth	July
Bainbridge In Bloom Garden Tour	July
Outdoor Music Festival	August
Summer Studio Tour	August
Studio Tour/Christmas in the Country	November
Harvest Fair	October
Mochi Tsuke	December

Belfair

Belfair Summerfest	June
Taste of Hood Canal	August

Bremerton

Concerts in the Park	June
Concerts in the Park	July
"Fireworks, Sinclair Inlet"	July
Kitsap Fair & Rodeo	August
Concerts in the Park	August
Blackberry Festival	September

Clallam Bay/Sekiu

Clallam Bay/Sekiu Fun Days	July

Elma

Grays Harbor County Fair	September

Forks

Rain Festival	April
Fourth of July/Fireworks	July
Heritage Days	October

Gig Harbor

Blessing of the Fleet	June
Maritime Gig Festival	June
Winterfest	November

Grayland

Annual Driftwood Show	March
Windrider Kite Festival	July
30 Miles of Junque Garage Sale	September
Cranberry Harvest Festival	October

Hoodsport

Hood Canal Oyster Bite	April
Celebrate Hoodsport 4th of July	July
Hoodsport SCUBA Festival	September
Annual Holiday Festival & Bazaar	November

Hoquiam

Grays Harbor Shorebird Festival	April
Loggers Play Day	September

Kingston

Fourth of July	July
Bluegrass Festival	September

Lake Quinault

Lake Quinault Bike Ride	July

Neah Bay

Makah Days	August

North Beach

Come Have a Ball on the North Beach	January
Come Have a Ball on the North Beach	February
Come Have a Ball on the North Beach	March
State Route 109 Garage Sale	April
North Coast Sky Painters Fun Fly	August

Olalla

Summer Bluegrass Festival	August

Ocean Shores

Sunlover's Indoor Beach Bash	January
Write on the Beach	January
Photography & Fine Arts Show	April
International Kite Challenge	June
Northwest Sand Sculpture Open	June
Sand & Sawdust Festival	June
Sun & Surf Run - H.O.G.S.	July
Dixieland Jazz Festival	November

Pacific Beach

Sandcastle Contest	September
Up Your Wind Kite Festival	September

Port Angeles

Juan de Fuca Festival	May
Fourth of July/Fireworks	July
Clallam County Fair	August
Strait Bluegrass Festival	September

Port Gamble

North Kitsap Arts & Crafts Show	July
Medieval Faire	June
Country Christmas	December

Port Hadlock

Port Hadlock Days	July

Port Ludlow

Port Ludlow Days	September

Port Orchard

Seagull Calling Festival	May
Fathoms o' Fun/Fireworks July 4	June/July
South Kitsap Garden Tour	June
Festival by the Bay & Great Ball Race	August
Mosquito Fleet Maritime Festival	September

Port Townsend

Chamber Music Festival	February
Victorian Festival	March
Kitemakers' Conference	March
Port Townsend Playwrights' Festival	March
Port to Port Regatta	April
Rhododendron Festival	May
Jefferson County Secret Garen Tour	June
Festival of American Fiddle Tunes	July
Jazz Port Townsend	July
Country Blues Festival	August
Jefferson County Fair	August
Wooden Boat Festival	September
Quilting By the Sound	September
Kinetic Sculpture Race	October

Poulsbo

Kitsap Quilters Show	February
Viking Fest	May
Skandia Midsommerfest	June
Fireworks on the Fjord	July
Arts by the Bay	August
Septemberfest	September
Renaissance Nights	September
Annual Lutefisk Dinner	October
Yule Fest	Nov/Dec

Quilcene/Brinnon

Salmon Derby	February
Heritage Days	April
ShrimpFest	May
Olympic Music Festival	June
Quilcene Fair & Parade	September

Sequim

Irrigation Festival	May

Jazz Festival	June	Strawberry Festival	July
Lavender Festival	July	Holiday Open House	December
Dungeness River Festival	September	**Westport**	
Shelton		World Class Crab Races & Crab Feed	April
Mason County Forest Festival	June	Annual Blessing of the Fleet	May
Mason County Fair	July	Booming Bay Fireworks Display	July
Oysterfest	October	Elk River Challenge	July
Silverdale		Northwest Longboard Surfing Classic	July
Whaling Days	July	Annual Seafood Festival	August
Christmas Tree Lighting	December	International Nautical Chainsaw Carving	August
Suquamish		Brady's Annual Oyster Feed	August
Native American Art Fair	April	Westport Art Festival	August
Fireworks on the Slab	July	30 Miles of Junque Garage Sale	September
Chief Seattle Days	August		
Vashon Island			
Spring Fling	April		
Fourth of July/Fireworks	July		

You have probably heard of the Pacific Northwest's reputation for rain, and there is no denying the fact that we do get quite a lot of it. However, most of it comes in the form of drizzle or mist during seemingly endless days of gray winter skies. Hard, driving rains are not the norm, and lightning and thunder are rare, and usually happen only in winter or spring.

The average annual amount of rainfall in inches is actually about the same as places in the eastern part of the country, even less, for example, than Chicago. It's just that ours compresses into a 6 to 7 month period and theirs averages out over the whole 12 months.

Sometimes fate plays a cruel joke on us and it rains all summer. We had two of them recently during the El Niño and La Niña years, but this is the exception. During the days between July 4 and October 1, we have our dry season (all the native vegetation has evolved to handle it), and often it will not rain at all. Those are the days of outdoor weddings, picnics, festivals and other open air events, and a lot of lawn watering and garden irrigation. They are also the days when people worry about forest fires, and so outdoor fires, including campfires, are banned.

It seldom gets really hot here; a day over 70° F is considered a heat wave. And almost every evening you'll need a sweater or jacket. But that also ensures comfortable sleeping conditions. You'll notice an almost complete absence of air conditioners.

In the Puget Sound area, unless it is actually raining, the humidity is generally a good deal lower than places on the East Coast or Midwest for the comparable time of year. The Olympic Mountains filter out a good deal of the moisture-bearing air and force it to dump on the rain forest (some 140 inches per year), resulting in lower humidity for the air that gets past them.

But, on the other hand, in the lowlands it doesn't really get what the rest of the country considers cold, either. On Bainbridge Island, we usually get by with a wool sweater throughout the winter. Some winters it doesn't get below freezing, but we may have an occasional light dusting of snow. Every several years we may get an unexpected cold snap (a cold snap is anything below freezing) and even a heavy snow. Generally, extreme weather is infrequent and a total surprise, especially to local drivers.

The climates at sea level and in the mountains can vary dramatically, especially in winter. It is quite common to have rock 'em - sock 'em blizzards in the passes adding to the eighty plus inches of base snow, while a light rain falls on bare pavement at sea level. We've seen 20 feet of snow in the parking lot at Hurricane Ridge.

Winter weather reports always include the current freezing elevation. But *any trip* into wilderness backcountry at any time of year warrants packing clothing for virtually any kind of weather, not to mention the 10 Essentials (see page 106.)

Windstorms are also a rarity, but when they come, they are liable to be monumental. (In other areas of the world, they are known as hurricanes or typhoons -- in the spirit of understatement, we call them "windstorms") We name them after the holidays when they traditionally tend to occur, like the "Columbus Day Storm", the "Thanksgiving Storm" and the "Good Friday Storm". They have been known to take out bridges, as in the famous movie footage of the Tacoma Narrows Bridge, "Galloping Gertie", in 1942. A windstorm also destroyed the Hood

Canal Bridge (see Chapter 13) and a section of the Evergreen Point floating bridge on Lake Washington.

Cloudy days are very common east of the Olympics, as moisture from the Sound rises, or storms come in from the coast. On the coast, the weather can change rather quickly, with storms or squalls appearing suddenly. In the spring and fall there can be quite a bit of fog in both places.

If you listen to local weather reports, you will hear some special vocabulary items unique to our region. "Rain turning to showers" is one such enigmatic phrase. We sometimes tease visitors, insisting that if you pay really close attention, you can see the exact point at which this occurs. Another is "sun breaks". This means that the sun may peek out between the clouds a couple of times that day. "Black ice" refers to moisture on the roadways from rain or dew freezing into an invisible and potentially deadly, slick surface. Take it very seriously.

What to pack? The "layered look" is what local resident and internationally known travel expert Rick Steves recommends for his *Europe Through the Back Door* tours, and it applies here at home as well. Cotton or silk turtlenecks with sweaters and/or fleece vest, and a hooded wind breaker or parka with comfortable slacks or skirt and plenty of extra socks, tights or leggings and ultra-comfortable shoes. This is Eddie Bauer country, even in the city, so you can leave the feather boa, black tie and cummerbund at home. If your want to pass for a local, omit the umbrella, but bring a waterproof jacket with hat or hood. "Gortex" is king here.

There is a very good chance that the weather will be fine during your stay west of Puget Sound. If it isn't, you have the opportunity to appreciate the natural forces that make our region literally a cold jungle with some of the fastest-renewing vegetation on earth.

The first chart shows the statistics for the Puget Sound area. Across from Seattle, they are similar at the lower elevations, but colder the higher you go. Rainfall is considerably less on the northeastern side of the Olympic Mountains, much, much more on the southwest side.

Puget Sound Area

Rainfall in inches	Average High	Average Low	% of Sunny Days
Jan	6	45	36	28%
Feb	4	50	38	34%
Mar	3.5	52	39	42%
Apr	2.5	58	42	47%
May	1.5	65	48	52%
Jun	1.5	69	53	49%
Jul	1	75	56	63%
Aug	1	74	56	56%
Sep	2	64	53	53%
Oct	3.5	60	47	37%
Nov	5.5	51	41	28%
Dec	6.5	47	42	23%
Total	38.5			

This chart shows the rainfall and temperature for Forks and the coastal rainforest. The average annual rainfall is almost 10 feet a year! If people in Seattle have T-shirts that say "Seattlites don't tan -- they rust!", what must the T-shirts say in Forks? "My Volkswagen beetle looks like a chia pet"?

Sequim is the other side of the coin. In the "rain shadow" on the northeast side of the Olympic range, it receives much less rainfall than the rainforest, or even Puget Sound. Sequim was the first agricultural community in the state to develop an irrigation system. Pretty amazing, when you consider how dry the eastern portion of Washington is.

Forks Area - The Rain Forest

	Rainfall in inches	Record Rainfall	Average High	Average Low
Jan	17.4	40.1	45	33
Feb	14.3	32.7	49	34
Mar	12.8	29.7	52	35
Apr	8.5	17.9	57	38
May	5.3	14.4	63	42
Jun	3.5	10.6	67	47
Jul	2.3	9.5	71	49
Aug	2.4	13.5	72	50
Sep	4.8	17.6	69	47
Oct	11.8	29.4	60	42
Nov	16.1	35.3	51	37
Dec	18.8	41.7	46	34
Total	118.0			

Sequim - The "Rain Shadow"

	Rainfall in inches	Average High	Average Low
Jan	3.1	46	32
Feb	1.1	48	31
Mar	1.4	51	33
Apr	1.0	55	36
May	1.1	60	43
Jun	1.1	64	47
Jul	0.6	68	50
Aug	0.5	70	49
Sep	0.6	66	44
Oct	1.8	57	38
Nov	2.1	58	35
Dec	1.7	47	31
Total	16.0		

TThese Chambers of Commerce and Visitor Centers are listed in their respective chapters, but it seemed a good idea to put them all together in one place here.

Bainbridge Island Chamber of Commerce, 590 Winslow Way E, 206/842-3700, *bainbridgechamber.com*

Bremerton Area Chamber of Commerce, 301 Pacific Ave, 360/479-3579, *bremertonchamber.org*

Clallam Bay - Sekiu Chamber of Commerce, 360/963-2339 *sekiu.com clallambay.com*

Elma Chamber of Commerce, 117 N Third St, PO Box 798, 360/482-3055 *elmachamber.org*

Forks Chamber of Commerce, 800/443-6757, 360/374-2531, *forkswa.com*

Gig Harbor Chamber of Commerce, 3302 Harborview Drive, 253/851-6865 *gigharborchamber.com*

Grays Harbor Chamber of Commerce and Visitors Center (Aberdeen & Hoquiam), 506 Duffy St, Aberdeen 360/532-1924, *tourismgraysharbor.com*

Hoh Rainforest Visitors Center 360/374-6925

Hurricane Ridge Visitor Center 360/452-4501 For snow and road conditions 360/565-3131

Kalaloch Visitor Center, 360/962-2283

Kingston Chamber of Commerce, 11212 Hwy 104, 360/297-3813, *kingstonchamber.org*

Kitsap Peninsula Visitor and Convention Bureau 360/297-8200, *visitkitsap.com. Hours:* Visitor Information Center: 9-5 daily in summer, less on weekends in winter

North Mason Chamber of Commerce, Visitor Information Center & Mary E. Theler Community Center, Belfair, 360/275-5548, *northmasonchamber.com*

Ocean Shores Chamber of Commerce, 800/762-3224, 360/289-2451, *oceanshores.org*

Olympic National Park Visitor Center, 3002 Mt Angeles Rd & Race St, Port Angeles, 360/565-3130 *olympic.national-park.com*

Port Angeles Chamber of Commerce *portangeles.net/*

Port Orchard Chamber of Commerce 360/876-3505, 1014 Bay St Suite 8, *portorchard.com/chamber*

Port Townsend Chamber of Commerce 888/365-6978, 360/385-2722, *ptchamber.org*

Poulsbo Chamber of Commerce 19131 8th Ave NE, 360/779-4848, *poulsbochamber.com*

Quilcene-Brinnon Chamber of Commerce, 360/765-4999**,** *www.emeraldtowns.com*

Sequim Visitors Center, **Sequim/Dungeness Valley Chamber of Commerce,** 1192 E. Washington St 800/737-8462, 360/683-6197, *visitsun.com*

Shelton/Mason County Chamber of Commerce, 221 W Railroad Avenue, Suite 5 & 6, 800/576-2021 or 360/ 426-2021, *sheltonchamber.org*

Silverdale Chamber of Commerce 360/692-6800, info@silverdalechamber.com *silverdalechamber.com*

Vashon-Maury Island Chamber of Commerce 206/463-6217, *vashonchamber.com*

Washington Coast Chamber of Commerce, 2616A SR 109, Ocean City, WA, 800/286-4552, 360-289-4552, *washingtoncoastchamber.org*

Westport-Grayland Chamber of Commerce, 2985 S Montesano St, 800/345-6223, 360/268-9422, *westportgrayland-chamber.org*

The Pacific Northwest has some of the richest and varied wildlife in the world, and encoun- tering at least some of them becomes an everyday experience.

Bald eagles fly over our houses, blacktail deer munch our roses, black bear and racoons rummage in our compost piles and garbage cans, and cougars occasionally lurk just beyond the borders of our yards. Elk, who live in high altitudes during the summer, come down in winter and brazenly occupy towns like Brinnon and Sequim where grazing is plentiful and human residents eventually learn to coexist with them.

People who live near the water routinely see sea lions snoozing on their docks and sailboats and Orca (killer whales) chasing salmon. We live so intimately with these magnificent creatures that learning to exercise respect and caution is a part of our ongoing education.

Flora

Our land vegetation is among the most rapidly renewable in the whole world. If our lawn didn't get mowed for a year, there would be a small forest growing there in no time. In five years, it would be a big forest.

Douglas firs are our most common conifer, and although not as huge as the legendary Sequoias of California, a stand of old-growth firs is certainly impressive. The official state tree is the hemlock, but we think that's because Oregon had first pick. Red cedars, which grow in the wetter areas, have always been considered sacred by Native Americans. Many European- Americans share this respect. Red alder is the most abundant deciduous tree; they are leguminous, fixing nitrogen in the soil, and are among the first plants to come back after a forest fire. They grow amazingly fast and quickly reach 100 feet tall. Their natural lifespan is short, and they readily fall over in windstorms, becoming "nurse logs" and rapidly decomposing to feed others like firs and cedars. They supply us with firewood and burn quite fragrantly, hence their popularity for smoking foods.

Ron's favorite tree is the Pacific Madrone, with its smooth red bark, contorted trunk, large, leathery oval leaves and red berries. These trees usually grow on the southwest side of a hill.

Some of the most prolific vegetation are transplants from other places with no natural enemies here: Himalayan blackberry, Scotch broom, English ivy and holly. Many of *our* native wild plants are cultivated prizes for gardens in other mild climates like England: flowering currant, vine maple, Oregon grape, and kinnick-kinnick to name a few.

Wild Flowers and Alpine Meadows. Forget Julie Andrews and *The Sound of Music*. Don't go traipsing off the trails into the alpine meadows — delicate wildflowers survive under the harshest of conditions and don't need added stress from us.

You will see the most unusual shapes, colors, almost-alien life forms – don't pick them – they need every viable seed in place to survive.

Many of these flowers are specifically adapted to their extreme natural environments and may not make it in your garden anyway. Global warming is also having a negative impact on the plants, due to changes in rainfall, snow-pack and temperature conditions. Specially-collected seeds are available for purchase at Olympic National Park centers.

Mushrooms love the wet Pacific Northwest, and you may see many different kinds as you walk through a forest in any but the driest time of year. Some are deadly. Do not pick and eat wild mushrooms unless you *really* know what you are doing.

Fauna

Dolphins and Orcas are often seen in the northern part of Puget Sound, and on rarer occasions, gray whales.

Whales and dolphins of many kinds can be seen along the coast during the spring migration from early March to late May.

Since prehistoric times, salmon have been an important part of the local economy, and it's not hard to spot them leaping out of the water during spawning season. Almost everyone knows someone who fishes them for a living.

Some of the largest octopus in the world have been found in Puget Sound. We've heard tales of them crawling up on someone's beachfront and scaring the daylights out of them. If you could see underwater, you would be amazed at the bizarre and colorful marine life among the rocks and pilings. Not surprisingly, Puget Sound is a mecca for underwater divers.

Tidepools around the Sound, the Strait and the coast provide a peek into another world for those not willing to put on SCUBA gear. Here are some of the things you may see at low tide:

Several types of starfish, anemones, sea urchins in a wide assortment of shapes and colors, tube worms, sponges corals, sea squirts, and the world's largest barnacles.

Sea slugs (nudibranchs), sculpins, sole, flounder, various crabs and shrimp.

Intertidal vegetation includes kelp, wrack and other sea weeds, eelgrass and algae.

Limpets, winkles, whelks, sand dollars, sea snails, scallops, oysters, cockles and mussels, many varieties of clams, including the king of them all, the **geoduck** (pronounced "gooey-duck").

The world's largest burrowing bivalve lives right here in Puget Sound. The name comes from the Nisqually language (*gweduc*) and translates as "dig deep" — very appropriate for an animal that spends its entire life of 140 years or more buried three feet deep in beach mud or sand and can reach a weight of 20 pounds.

The "neck" or siphon extends up to 39 inches and together with the foot is too big to be completely retracted within the shell. The sight of the phallic siphon of a harvested geoduck sitting around in a local fish market is enough to make gentlemen exclaim and ladies swoon.

Ron and friends Jerry and Judie Elfendahl immortalized the geoduck in song in 1972 by authoring the "Gooey-Duck Song", now an official Washington State folksong:

Well, he hasn't got a front
And he hasn't got a back,
He doesn't know Donald
And he doesn't go "quack".

Dig a duck, dig a duck,
Dig a gooey-duck,
Dig a duck, dig a gooey-duck,
Dig a duck a day!

Large mammals include the black bear, cougar, Roosevelt elk, blacktail and mule deer. Roosevelt Elk were named for Teddy who made the Olympic Forest Reserve a national monument in 1909, not cousin Franklin D., who created the national park in 1938. Mountain goats can also be seen in the Olympics – they were introduced in the beginning of the twentieth century and now there are hundreds.

Resident smaller mammals include raccoons, the native red squirrel and Douglas squirrel (which are threatened by the interloping and more aggressive Eastern gray squirrel), river and sea otters, seals and sea lions, foxes, beavers, coyotes, and the very occasional skunk and opossum.

The Douglas squirrel or chickoree is an animal with attitude, despite its tiny size. It is the sentinel of the forest, announcing the arrival of strangers for the benefit of the rest of the neighborhood. The alarm cries ("Pyew! Pyew! Pyew!"), sometimes mistaken for bird calls, may be directed at you, a passing cat or other predator, or another intruding Douglas squirrel.

In the mountain meadows you will hear the whistles of, if not see, marmots. The Olympic Mountains have their own unique variety, probably separated from their Cascade kin during glaciation.

The Pacific Northwest is a magnet for birders in any season. Our mild climate means that many species live here year-round, and we are along the coastal flyway for others who come and go.

On the water there are eagles, osprey, coots, loons, many varieties of ducks and seagulls, sandpipers, blue heron, kingfishers and cormorants, and even puffins at the ocean shores.

Inland you may see bald eagles, red-tail hawks, ravens, juncos, towhees, chickadees, pine siskins, robins, mourning doves, owls, flickers and other woodpeckers, many wrens, finches, thrushes, warblers and grosbeaks, and redwing blackbirds with a slightly different accent than their eastern cousins.

The English sparrow, while ubiquitous in Seattle, is too much a city dweller to be interested in all but the most urban areas of the Kitsap or Olympic Peninsulas.

For a list of the top birding locations, go to **Appendix L, Favorite Birdwatching Areas.**

Reptiles and amphibians are represented with various frogs, toads, salamanders, and newts. We have turtles and several species of snakes, although none poisonous west of the Cascades.

Local insects include swallowtail and other species of butterflies, moths, dragonflies, solitary native bees like bumblebees and orchard mason bees, beetles and many others. Those giant mosquito-looking things are crane flies and do not bite. Local kids call them "mosquito eaters", but they don't do that, either. Unlike other parts of the U.S., the actual mosquito population, thankfully, is fairly sparse.

Slugs! No guide to our area would be complete without a short disseration on slugs. These land mollusks (think of them as snails without shells) abound in our damp climate. The yellow banana slug is one of the few native ones. Others have come from Europe and Asia, and can be found in brown, black, dark red, gray and leopard-spotted.

Like its snail kin, a slug secretes mucus from its foot and moves along on top of it. You can often see shimmering silver slime trails on the ground or on vegetation. Slug slime is so effective that slugs can navigate the edge of a razor blade!

Slugs are part of Nature's decomposition system, but the imported ones tend to like young garden plants all too well. The tongue or *radula* has more than 20,000 sharp teeth (which puts a shark to shame) and rasps the food source like a file. Slugs will eat just about anything —plant material, dead slugs and, as we can attest to, cat food.

Slugs are hermaphroditic, but it requires two of them to mate to produce offspring. The details of their courtship are far too bizarre and licentious to include here.

Copper is like Kryptonite to slugs. It carries a slight electrical charge, which is transmitted to them through the moisture of their slime. Copper barriers afford some hope to beleaguered gardeners.

The most notorious local Northwest species is the fabled Sasquatch, also known as "Bigfoot"; however, you're not likely to run into one. But if you do, you could become famous, especially if you have your camera handy.

Potentially Dangerous Wildlife

Bears. Despite having been the model for the Teddy Bear, black bears should never be underestimated.

Generally bears are as happy to avoid us as we are them. However, there are two situations in which bears can be very dangerous: 1) if there is a female bear with cubs, and 2) if a bear has become habituated to humans and looks up on our habitat (campground?) as a source of food.

A friend of ours was driving home one afternoon on a side road and had to stop his car for what appeared to be a black dog lying in the middle of the lane. He rolled down his window to yell at it, and discovered it was a bear! So he rolled up his window really quickly.

Do not EVER try to feed a bear, even if you think you are safe in your car. Once a window is rolled down a crack, they can break it so fast you won't know what happened.

If you are camping by car, lock **ALL** your food in the car at night – in the trunk if possible. Do not allow the smallest piece of gum in your tent. If you have a camping icebox, put that in the car, too. Bears can open them like we open tin cans.

If you are camping on foot, bring 50 feet of rope along to suspend any edibles high in a tree and well away from your tent. Many people hang a bell on their pack to make noise to warn any bears away.

Black bears are smaller than grizzlies, but they can still run faster than a race horse (30 mph), and they weigh a whole lot more than you do. Take precautions: make plenty of noise on the trail; if a bear menaces you, don't run, act small, play dead.

Cougars. With cougars, the opposite is true – they are less likely to attack something larger and unknown. Don't run, stand and face them – act big, make lots of noise and fight back.

Elk & Deer. These animals can definitely have attitudes, backed up by antlers and sharp hooves, despite what you think you know from *Bambi*. Many have become way too habituated to humans for your comfort. Avoid close encounters, especially in the fall during rutting (breeding) season.

Deer often collide with automobiles, spelling disaster for all parties. Drive carefully in known deer areas, especially in twilight hours – morning and evening – when these animals tend to move around a lot.

Remember, if one deer or elk crosses the road in front of your car, several more may follow.

Swans. This may sound silly, but we have heard from several guests visiting the Bloedel Reserve (plus Mickey's own childhood experience) that swans can be very aggressive. They can be belligerent, in the same manner as domestic geese. Swans are lovely and graceful — at a distance. Don't mess with swans.

We have the last glacier to thank for the Puget Sound basin. Around 11,000 years ago it carved out Puget Sound, the Hood Canal and the Strait of Juan de Fuca first through scouring and then through the melting of tons of ice.

Western Washington has been in a big squeeze for millions of years. We are part of the larger geologically-active Pacific Rim, with its "Ring of Fire" of volcanos and earthquakes.

Three tectonic plates come together at our coast: the US Continental plate, the Pacific plate under the ocean, and the Juan de Fuca plate, between the other two.

The collision of these earth masses has totally transformed the area over time, creating the Olympic Mountains by uplift (basically an accordion fold of rock and soil) as the Juan de Fuca plate slides under the Continental plate in the area along the coast of British Columbia, Washington and Northern Oregon known as the Cascadia Subduction Zone.

The pressure and friction underground creates molten lava, which is forced up through the volcanos of the Cascade Mountains.

The upside of this geophysical activity are hot springs, like those found at Sol Duc Hot Springs.

Even though our geological clock generally ticks very slowly, once in a while the alarm goes off.

Earthquakes

No wonder we get a few earthquakes now and then! Every 25 to 30 years or so, we get a 6-7 point near-surface quake. Every 300-1200 years we get a bigger subduction quake.

Don't let seismic events be a concern. There have been far fewer casualties in the last 50 years due to earthquakes and volcanos than there are in a week of normal traffic in New York City. We just had the biggest quake in 35 years (Nisqually Quake, 2002), which means we should still be good for another 30 or so.

Want to have some fun? Ask a bunch of locals where they were during the last big quake. At our house, some workmen were 30 feet up on our roof repairing our chimney and barely managed to hang on.

What to do in the odd chance you experience an earthquake? Outdoors – move away from buildings, power lines and large trees. Indoors – move away from windows, get under tables, beds, or stand in an interior doorway.

Tsunamis

A *tsunami*, or tidal wave, is the result of an earthquake somewhere else, probably on the Pacific Ocean floor or the coast of Asia. This earth movement can result in a wall of water – sometimes several stories high – slamming against our coastline.

Communities along the Washington coast have developed tsunami warning systems so that residents and visitors have the opportunity to reach high ground. Be aware of and follow signs in coastal areas.

History

Once upon a time, about 800 million years ago ("m.y.a."), the west coast of the Pacific Northwest was basically what is now the western border of Idaho. There was only one supercontinent, Pangea, which started to break up about 245 m.y.a. Volcanic eruptions in the Atlantic Ridge and in the Pacific started to force the continental plates apart.

The Pacific Plate and Juan de Fuca Plate are located west and east, respectively, of the volcanically active Juan de Fuca Ridge, some 200 miles off the shore of the Olympic Peninsula.

As volcanoes erupted creating ridges in the ocean floor, the materials flowed in either direction, causing movement of both plates. The Juan de Fuca plate was forced up against and under the Continent Plate.

Sooner or later, the North American continent, moving west, began to encounter newly formed Pacific volcanic islands moving east, which started to pile up against the continent, adding mass and discrete assemblages of similar rocks, sometimes hundreds of square miles in size, called *terranes*. The first major terrane landed about 175 m.y.a.

As each of these terranes piled up first against Idaho and then against each other, fault lines developed between them.

One such terrane was the Crescent Formation, a gigantic slab of basalt oceanic crust that was formed 50 to 60 m.y.a. Its name comes from outcroppings first seen around Lake Crescent, and also from the crescent shape it makes as it wraps around the northern, eastern and southern sides of the current Olympic Peninsula.

This rock originally was formed in eruptions on the ocean floor. It is part of the early Eocene lava which stretches from southern Vancouver Island, British Columbia to the Coast Range of Oregon.

The Crescent Formation docked against the continent during the Eocene epoch, about 35 m.y.a., and was subsequently pressured by more material from the west, causing the basalt to be upended and accumulate to a thickness of 10 miles, making it one of the thickest basalt formations in the world.

The motion and pressure continued, and the heavy crust of the Juan de Fuca tectonic plate continued to dive, or *subduct*, beneath the continental plate.

However, ocean sedimentary rocks, being lighter than volcanic rocks and the mantle, then floated up from the subduction trench and onto the continental plate, and were accordion-folded in the process, creating the peaks of the Olympic range (*Olympic Core*). Recent findings show that the Juan de Fuca Plate has subducted so far east as to be under the western portions of Kitsap County; i.e., east of the Hood Canal.

The Olympic Mountains themselves are very young by geological standards, having first begun to form only 15 million years ago. They are some of the youngest high mountains in the U.S.

The Puget Sound Lowland was formed by a combination of fault action and glaciation. Blocks of land dropped along fault lines, creating depressions.

To this day, shallow earthquakes continue to cause land to rise and fall along faults — the south end of Bainbridge Island experienced one such sudden uplift of 15 feet about 1,100 years ago. Lahars, mudflows from the Cascade volcanoes, also contributed to the composition of the eastern shore of the Sound.

Advancing glaciers filled the depressions, scoured them further, and left large deposits of rock and soil debris called *moraines.*

There were at least 4 great ice ages, and many smaller ones, with the last one reaching south of Olympia and ending only about 11,000 years ago.

The several large glaciers which remain in the Olympic Mountains today once filled the western river basins of the Peninsula, in some cases all the way to the ocean. Today the glaciers come down to about 5000 feet above sea level.

The erosion by glaciers differs from the erosion by water. Water tends to cut deeply and quickly, causing a V-shaped valley. The mass of glacial ice, on the other hand, causes pressure laterally as well as downhill, carving out a U-shaped valley.

Introducing the Rocks Across the Sound

Sandstone: formed from grains of quartz, feldspar, mica, other iron- and magnesium silicates. Under pressure became semischist.

Shale: formed from oceanic mud – clay minerals, quartz, feldspar, mica. Under pressure became slate and phyllite.

Conglomerate and Sedimentary Breccia: Sands and muds including pebbles and cobbles.

Basalt: Formed from molten lava. Underwater lava flow produces rounded masses called pillows, black or dark green in color. Broken up pieces form volcanic breccia. Under pressure became greenstone. Lavas on the surface cooled and shrank, developing cracks that allowed the formation of polygonal vertical basalt columns.

Quartz: Under pressure from movements of the earth's crust the rocks metamorphosized and quartz formed to filled the empty spaces

The Major Rivers or Drainage Basins of the Olympic Peninsula:

East
Dosewallips
Duckabush
Hamma Hamma
Skokomish

North
Elwha
Dungeness

West
Sol Duc
Bogachiel
Hoh
Queets
Quinault

South
Humptulips
Wynoochee
Skokomish (South Fork)

Places to See Geological Features Firsthand:

East
Toe Jam Hill, Bainbridge Island - late Holocene fault scarp on the Seattle Fault - Fort Ward Hill Rd. and Toe Jam Hill Rd.

Waterman Fault, ½ mile north of Manchester State Park, Port Orchard

Road cuts along west side of **Hood Canal** - basalt columns.

Dosewallips Valley - the road to the Dosewallips Campground passes under a huge cliff of pillow basalt. This area is the thickest part of the Crescent Formation, probably over 10 miles thick.

Lake Cushman - formed by a glacier and enhanced by a dam. Staircase

North
Deer Park Road - banks reveal layers of stratified rock sandstone and shale in alternate layers. Formed from sand and mud in the ocean 40 - 60 million years ago.

Dungeness Spit - combination of glacial deposits from the Dungeness River plus sea currents. One of the largest natural sandspits in the world, it is constantly reshaping itself.

Elwha River Road - South of Highway 101, the road and the river cut through a notch in the basalt. More basalt outcroppings can be seen along the river's west bank. Observation Point provides a good vantage to see the overall glacier-modified landscape as well as the opportunity to look at sandstone deposits rich in mica.

Hurricane Ridge - the road to the Visitor Center features basalt pillows in the road cuts. The trail to Hurricane Hill features rocks that once were on the floor of the ocean. Shortly after the trail begins, there are outcrops of turbidites (folded sedimentary shale and sandstone). Sandstone with quartz can be seen just past the crossing with the Little River Trail. As the trail goes into meadows, you can see cliffs of pillow basalt, which mark the border between the Crescent Formation and the Olympic Core. The summit of the hill has more pillow basalt.

Lake Crescent - the lake was carved out by the glacier, then a landslide (probably caused by an earthquake) at the eastern end sealed off the bottom section as Lake Sutherland. You can climb to the top of Mt. Storm King, a basalt massif. Rock cuts along the highway reveal pillow basalt.

Spruce Railroad Trail, Lake Crescent - Harrigan Point has a great example of a *Bouma Sequence*, a sedimentary deposit which has also displays evidence of disturbance by fault action. At Devils Point there are large breccias, and a half mile beyond is a section of what was once sea floor, with basalt pillows.

Sol Duc Falls and Hot Springs - Sol Duc Falls cuts through upended sandstone deposits. The hot springs, while not situated directly over the Calawah fault (running along the edge of the Crescent Formation basalt horseshoe) are close enough to it to take advantage of the heat.

West

Cape Flattery - the bedrock is called *breccia,* a concrete like substance made of sand with angular pebbles and larger rocks included. Where the brecchia has been carved away by the wave action, you can see some of the larger rock inclusions, which are several feet in diameter.

Sea stacks and islands like Tatoosh and James Islands along the northern section of the coast are what remain of ancient headlands worn away by the sea.

Lake Ozette - was formed by a glacial moraine. At the time of its formation, it was a great deal farther inland from the coast.

Point of the Arches - the oldest rocks are at least 144 million years old and are probably eroded from the old continent upon which the current peninsula now rests. Take the trail to Shi Shi Beach and turn north. There is also *gabbro* white feldspar with black hornblende spots) along the cliffs south of the point, which can be reached at low or very low tide.

Hoh River - once this wide U-shaped valley contained a glacier that reached all the way to the sea. Modern experience of the Muir Glacier in Alaska's Glacier Bay gives us a sense of what that must have been like. Most of the rock material here is gravel deposited by the glacier, made up of the metamorphosed sandstone and slate that were once the sea floor. At the head of the valley, the Hoh Glacier and Blue Glacier still remain. You can sometimes hear the thunder-like sound produced by falling ice.

Lake Quinault - is a U-shaped valley eventually dammed by moraine from its own glacier. Merriman Falls, on the Enchanted Valley trail, plummets down the steep side of the valley. The gorge at Pony Bridge provides an opportunity to see layers of slate and sandstone.

South

Wynoochee River - U-shaped glacial valley.

Westport Dunes - sediments from the Columbia River have been sweeping northward so that the landform has been increasing. The lighthouse once stood on the edge of the sea.

G WELCOME TO THE WILDERNESS

This travel guide is generally designed for the traveler in a car who will make occasional stops and venture along well-marked trails. One thing to keep in mind – the native people who have lived here for at least 10,000 years kept to the waterways or a few well-worn paths, and did not venture inland indiscriminately.

In a rain forest, it quickly becomes difficult to find reliable points of reference. Basically, most trees look alike. And for many days of the year, the location of the sun or stars in the sky is not available to help with navigation.

If you are following a well-marked main path to a well-documented target (waterfall, beach, etc.), great. But if you reach a fork in a path and decide to strike out in one direction or the other, or you choose a longer outing, you need to, as the Scouts say, BE PREPARED:

The most serious, life-threatening danger in the Pacific Northwest is getting cold and wet.

The second-most serious, life-threatening danger is getting lost, which will probably also eventually involve getting cold and wet.

It is critical to avoid hypothermia, the condition in which cool or cold (and by no means necessarily freezing) external temperatures, often magnified by moisture, cause the human body to no longer be able to maintain its core temperature of 98.6 degrees Fahrenheit.

An incredible number of search-and-rescue efforts are in progress in this area at any time throughout the year. Mountaineers, 4x4 vehicle owners, search dog people, Eagle Scouts, as well as National Ski Patrollers in winter, county sheriffs and local police with back-up from Army and Navy helicopters -- these volunteers and professionals are kept very busy rescuing the often not very-well-prepared public in our vast wilderness areas. Very simple preparations will keep you from being the focal point of one of these rescue efforts.

The **Mountaineers**, a non-profit organization based in Seattle, is dedicated to preserving the wilderness and enjoying the outdoors safely. Members can take part in educational courses and organized actvities. The club offers a wealth of information about all kinds of wilderness recreation on their web site and in numerous books and publications.

The Mountaineers and other wilderness adventurers have devised a list of the **Ten Essentials** to carry with you *any time* you take a hike:

1. Extra clothing needs to be based on the idea of increasing layers of warmth, plus moisture and wind resistance. Cotton denim has little or no insulating qualities, especially when wet. Wool or synthetics are a much better choice. Extra socks are very important. A plastic rain poncho, available at most local supermarkets or hardware stores, is an inexpensive investment.

2. Extra food and water. Should be light-weight and very concentrated in carbohydrates, fats and proteins. Nut bars, protein bars, sugars and candy are ideal and, for once, chocolate is good for you.

Water: A fast-moving mountain stream is pure and safe to drink - right? WRONG! You will be putting yourself at risk for *Girardia* and other bacterial infections. Also, glacial water may contain dangerous mineral particles that would be the equivalent of drinking finely ground glass.

Bring bottled water, or boil any water or snow that you collect. Specifically-designed portable water filters can also be used.

3. Sunglasses reduce the strain on your eyes, and help you from becoming tired. They are very important in snow conditions, helping reduce the possibility of snow-blindness.

4. A sharp knife, preferably of the Swiss Army multi-function variety, has a multitude of uses.

5. Fire starter - you can't EVER count on dry firewood in the Pacific Northwest. A small can of Sterno and a candle will go a long way. Also, you can pick up a small pack of fire-starter in most grocery stores.

6. A very basic first aid kit can prevent foot blisters, help with insect bites, and accommodate sprains and other misfortunes.

7. Matches in a waterproof container are a must. A butane lighter also works, as long as it is full.

8. Flashlight with extra bulb and batteries. Moving around in unknown territory in the dark is no picnic. It can also be used for signaling, and for scaring off predator animals.

9. Map. If you are doing ANY kind of back country travel, you need the detailed maps from the United States Geodetic Survey (USGS). They are available at the Olympic National Park Visitor Center in Port Angeles, at Ranger Stations, and at other vendors including Internet sites.

10. Compass. Did you know that True North and Magnetic North are two different things? True North is a geographical reference: the place where the Big N is indicated on a map. Magnetic North is REALITY -- where a compass actually points to and is determined by the state of the earth's electromagnetic field depending on your location on the planet.

In the Pacific Northwest, a compass will register Magnetic North **a full 20 degrees** to the east of True North. This can really mess you up if you are trying to use a compass to follow a map. The solution is to get a compass that allows you to adjust it for the declination — that is, the difference between True North and Magnetic North.

The Mountaineers
300 Third Ave West, Seattle, Wa 98119, 206/284-6310, *mountaineers.org*

Mountaineers Bookstore Online
mountaineersbooks.org

if you are looking for the usual national restaurant chains, you will find them well-represented in Bremerton, Poulsbo, Silverdale, Sequim, Port Angeles, and Aberdeen/Hoqiam.

We prefer in this publication whenever possible to celebrate locally-owned establishments with creativity and originality using locally-harvested ingredients.

We would also like to include those restaurants offering extensive and innovative vegetarian options.

This list is not all-inclusive, and we have not personally dined at all of these establishments, but have relied on general reputation and experiences of visitors. Also, this information may go out of date sooner than we can print a new edition of this book.

Please check with the local chamber of commerce/visitor information center (or their web site) for the most comprehensive and up-to-date listings and recommendations.

Aberdeen-Hoquiam

Billy's Bar & Grill, 322 E. Heron Street, 360/533-7144 Local favorite. 1906 building with unique back bar

Bridges Restaurant, 112 N. G Street, 360/532-6563 Steak & Seafood; 2 banquet rooms, separate lounge

Duffey's Restaurant, (2 locations) 1605 Simpson Av, 360/532-3842 & 1212 E. Wishkah St, 360/538-0606, Family dining

Mallard's Bistroe & Grill,118 E. Wishkah St, 360/532-0731, Fine dining

Parma Italian,116 W Heron, 360/532-3166 Authentic Northern Italian cuisine

Sidney's Restaurant, 512 W Heron, 360/533-0296 Full service menu; seafood and steak

Bainbridge Island

Bainbridge Waterfront Thai Cuisine, 330 Madison Av S, 206/780-2403 Friendly service, find food, great view

Bainbridge Sushi House, 108 Winslow Wy W, 206/780-9424 Chef from Japan, many many types of sushi

Bistro Pleasant Beach, 241 Winslow Wy W, 206/842-4347 Mediterranean cuisine

Cafe Nola, 101 Winslow Wy E, 206/842-3822 European, especially Italian, bistro fare

Casa Rojas, 403 Madison Av N, Suite 100, 206/855-7999 Authentic regional Mexican cuisine

Chili Cosmo's, 114 Madison Av S, 206/780-9053 Burritos and other fast lunch items

Colagreco's Italian Style Deli, 278 Winslow Wy E, Ste 206, 206/780-5354

Doc's Marina Grill, 403 Madison Av S, 206/842-8339 Family dining -- pastas and seafood

Four Swallows, 481 Madison Av N, 206/842-3397 Elegant Italian & American cuisine

Harbour Pub, 231 Parfitt Wy SW, 206/842-0969 Pub grub and microbrews at the marina

Isla Bonita, 316 Winslow W E, 206/780-9644 Authentic Mexican cuisine

Island Grill, 321 High School Rd, 206/842-9037 Steak and seafood

Islay Manor (formerly Ruby's), 4569 Lynwood Center Rd, 206/780-9303 Country French inspired NW cuisine

Mon Elisa's, 450 Winslow Wy E, 206/780-3233, Homemade pastas, salads, desserts

San Carlos, 279 Madison Av N, 206/842-1999 Southwestern & Mexican cuisine

Sawadty Thai, 8770 Fletcher Bay Rd, 206/780-2429 One of the best in the greater Seattle area

Simon's Chinese, 403 Madison Av N, Suite 150, 206/855-1845 Hunan, Szechuan & Mandarin cuisine

Winslow Way Cafe, 122 Winslow Way E, 206/842-0517
Steak, seafood, pasta, gourmet pizza

Via, 403 Madison Av N, 206/780-3888, Italian

Belfair

China Capital Restaurant, 23320 State Route 3, 360/275-4444, Cantonese, Szechuan, Mandarin

Fiesta Mexican Restaurant, 23720 NE State Route 3 (Log Cabin Plaza) 360/275-9392, Regional specialties.

Hank's Country Inn Restaurant, NE 22540 State Route 3, Belfair (near State Route 106 intersection) 360/275-3933 Full-service restaurant.

Ni-Thai-Na, 22421 State Route 3, 360/ 275-9460 Thai specialties

Old Clifton Town Deli & Bakery, 23690 NE State Route 3, 360/275-4966 Casual and specialties

Seabeck Pizza, 11 NE Old Belfair Highway, 360/275-2657 Pizza and specialties.

Silver Moon Resort, 4071 North Shore Road, 360/275-2657 Casual dining

Teriyaki Wok, 23961 NE State Route 3, 360/275-1111 Oriental cuisine.

Bremerton

Boat Shed, 101 Shore Dr (under the north side of the Manette Bridge), 360/377-2600 Seafood, accessible by boat

Noah's Ark, 1516 6th St, 360/377-8100
14 different gourmet burgers, Philly cheese steaks, gyros

Panda Inn Mongolian Restaurant 5050 Wheaton Wy E, 360/479-2732 Mongolian grill & Chinese cuisine

Brinnon

The Compass Rose, Hwy 101, 360/796-3553

Geoduck Cafe, Hwy 101, 360/796-4430

Halfway House Restaurant, Hwy 101, 360/796-4715

Seabeck Pizza, Hwy 101, 360/796-4611

Clallam Bay

Breakwater Inn, 15582 Hwy 113, Clallam Bay 360/ 963-2428 Breakfast, lunch, dinner, cocktails

Elma

El Paisano Taqueria, 201 W Eaton, 360/482-2328 Authentic Mexican tacos, tortillas, also vegetarian menu

Rusty Tractor, 602 E Young St, 360/482-3100 Family restaurant, old-fashioned cooking, breakfast, lunch & dinner

Saginaw's Deli & Diner, 101 South 3rd St, 360/ 482-8747 Ecletcic menu,cozy dining.

Savory Faire,135 Main St S, Montesano, 360/249-3701,European style bistro, homemade pastries and breads

Forks

The Coffee Shop, 241 Forks Ave, 360/374-6769 Breakfast, lunch, dinner

Golden Gate, 80 West A St, 360/ 374-5579 Shanghai Cuisine. Lunch, dinner, to go

Hungry Bear Cafe, 205860 Hwy 101 (15 mi N of Forks at Bear Creek), 360/327-3225, Breakfast, Lunch, Dinner, Beer & Wine

The In Place, 320 S. Forks Av, 360/374-4004 Breakfast, lunch, dinner, beer and wine

Pacific Pizza, 870 Forks Av S, 360/ 374-2626
Pizza, sandwiches, salad bar, beer and wine, delivery

Plaza Jalisco, 90 N Forks Av, 360/ 374-3108
Authentic Mexican lunch & dinner. Marguaritas

Raindrop Cafe, 111 South Forks Av, 360/ 374-6612
Breakfast, lunch, dinner

Smoke House Restaurant ,193161 Hwy 101, 360/ 374-6258
Lunch, dinner, salad bar, lounge

South North Garden, 140 Sol Duc Way, 360/ 374-9779
Chinese food, lunch, dinner, cocktails, to go

Subway Sandwiches, 490 North Forks Av, 360/374-2442
Hot and Cold Sandwiches

Sully's Drive-In, 220 North Forks Av, 360/374-5075
Burgers and pizza, fountain selections

Vagabond Cafe, 81 North Forks Av, 360/374-6904
Lunch, dinner, lounge

Gig Harbor

El Pueblito, 3226 Harborview Dr, 253/858-9077
Mexican

The Green Turtle, 2905 Harborview Dr, 253/851-3167 Waterfront dining, Pacific Rim cuisine

Le Bistro Coffee House, 4120 Harborview Dr, 253/851-1033 Quiche, bagels, wraps, desserts, variety of vegetarian offerings

Marco's Ristorante, 7707 Pioneer Wy, 253/858-2899 Italian food and wine

Shoreline Steak & Seafood Grill, 8827 N Harborview Dr, 253/853-6353 Steak, seafood, chicken, pasta, on the waterfront

Tides Tavern, 253/858-3982 Fish & chips, burgers, pizza

Grayland

Seastar, 1800 Ste Rt 105 S, 360/267-1011 Fresh seafood, salad bar

Tokeland Hotel & Restaurant, 100 Hotel Rd, Tokeland, 360/267-7006 Seafood

Hoh

Hard Rain Cafe, 5673 Upper Hoh Road (17 mi S& W of Forks on Hoh Rainforest Road), 360/374-9288 Lunch, grill, snacks

Hoodsport

Hoodsport Inn, Downtown Hoodsport, 360/877-6720 Steaks & seafoood, breakfast, lunch & dinner

Hoodsport Marina and Cafe, N 24080 Highway 101, Hoodsport. 360/877-9657 Waterfront dining, seafood specialty.

Hungry Bear Restaurant, 36830 N Hwy 101, Eldon, WA, 360/877-5527, Steaks, primes, seafood, home-style breakfasts

Skipper John's, 23490 North Highway 101, 360/877-5661 Seafood specialties, take-out.

The Tides, 27061 North Highway 101, 360/877-8921

Kalaloch

Kalaloch Lodge Dining Room, 157151 Hwy 101 (33 mi S of Forks), 360/962-2271 Breakfast, lunch, dinner, cocktails.

Keyport

Whiskey Creek Steakhouse, 1918 Washington St, 360/779-3481 Steak! Live music Tues & Thurs.

Kingston

Keeper's Cove Restaurant, Point Casino, 7989 Salish Lane NE, 866/547-6468, 360/297-0070 Menu or buffet, Native American specialties

Kingston Inn, 24886 Washington Blvd, 360/297-3373

Joy Luck Restaurant, 10978 St Hwy 104, 360/297-3342 Chinese

Main Street Ale House, 1 Block West of Ferry Dock, 360/297-0440

Sakura Teriyaki, 27099 Miller Bay Rd, 360/297-7676

Lake Quinault

Rainforest Resort Village, 516 South Shore Lake Quinault, 360/288-2535 Salmon, steak, seafood and spaghetti

Lake Quinault Lodge, 345 S. Shore Lake Quinault, 800/562-6672 Historic Roosevelt dining room, lake view

La Push

Three Rivers Resort, 7764 LaPush Rd (Hwy 110, 8 mi W of Forks), 360/374-5300 Hamburgers, espresso, fountain selections, beer/wine

Neah Bay

Makah Maiden, Bayview Av, Neah Bay, 360/645-2789 Breakfast,lunch, dinner

North Beach

Ocean Crest, SR 109 Box 7, Moclips, 800/684-8439 Elegant dining with ocean view, traditional NW cuisine.

Ocean Shores

Alec's By The Sea, 131 E Chance-A-La-Mer Ocean Shores, 360/289-4026 Family dining

Dugan's Pizza, 690 Ocean Shores Blvd, 360/289-2330, Old-style pizza and Italian cuisine

Galway Bay Bar & Grill, 676 Ocean Shores Blvd NE, 360/289-2300, Traditional Irish fare

Homeport Restaurant, 857 Point Brown Av NW, Ocean Shores, 360/289-2600 Steak, fresh seafood, salad bar

Lucky Dragon Restaurant, 860 Point Brown Av NE, Ocean Shores, 360/289-2868, Chinese food

Mr. Bis Diner, 698 Ocean Shores Blvd, 360/289-0399 1950s decor dining, breakfast, lunch and dinner

Shilo Inn, 707 Ocean Shores Blvd, Ocean Shores, 360/289-0567 Four star restaurant. Steak and seafood

Waves Restaurant, 491 Damon Pt. Road NW, 360/289-3440, Fine dining and lounge with a view of the ocean

Port Angeles

Bella Italia, 118 E. 1st, 360/457-6112, Italian Cuisine. bellaitaliapa.com

Bonny's Bakery, 215 S Lincoln, 360/457-3585 Bakery items, soups and sandwiches

Bushwhacker Seafood Restaurant, 1527 E. 1st, 360/457-4113 Steak, seafood and Northwest cuisine

C'est Si Bon, 23 Cedar Park Rd, 360/452-8888 French Cuisine with Northwest quality ingredients. *northolympic.com/cestsibon*

Cafe Garden, 1506 E 1st, 360/457-4611 Seafood, steak, pasta

Downriggers, 115 East Railroad Av, 360/452-2700 Seafood & steak, lunch & dinner, waterfront

Indian Oven Restaurant, 222 N Lincoln, 360/452-5170 House of exotic Indian food. Dine in or take out.

Tannhauser, 1135 E Front St, 360/452-5977. German cuisine.

Thai Peppers, 222 N. Lincoln (1 block from ferry), 360/452-4995 Lunches & Dinners, no MSG, variety of vegetarian dishes

Port Ludlow

Fireside at The Inn at Port Ludlow, One Heron Rd, 360/437-7000

Harbormaster Seafood & Spirits Restaurant, 55 Heron Rd, 360/437-7400 Seafood with a view

113

Port Orchard

JJ's on the Bay, Downtown off Bay St, 360/876-1445 Grilled seafood, chowder & salad, burgers & steaks

Mary Mac's Restaurant at McCormick Woods, 5155 McCormick Woods Dr SW, 360/895-0142

Victorian Rose Tea Room, 1130 Bethel Av, 360/876-5695 At Springhouse Dolls & Gifts

Port Townsend

Ajax Cafe, On the Waterfront, Port Hadlock, 360/385-3450 Winner of the Best Steak award for 6 years, fresh Northwest seafood, live music.

The Belmont, 925 Water St., 360/385-3007 The last 1880's waterfront restaurant and saloon. Elegant 4 star menu and wine list. *the-belmont.com/hotel.html*

Elevated Ice Cream Co & Candy Shop, 627 & 631 Water St, 360/385-1156. Homemade ice cream and other delights.

El Sarape Mexican Restaurant, 630 Water Street, 360/379-9343 Authentic Mexican food,

El Sombrero, 1230 Sims Way, 360/370-9287 Vegetarian specials.

Fins Coastal Cuisine, 1019 Water St (upstairs), 360/379-3474 Seafood, waterfront views, upstairs in the Flagship Landing Building. *thepublichouse.com*

Fountain Cafe, 920 Washington Street, 360/385-1364 For almost 20 years, PT's answer to the Moosewood Cafe.

Khu Larb Thai, 225 Adams, 360/385-5023 Traditional Thai

La Isla, 1145 Water St, 360/385-1714 Mexican Food. Waterfront near the ferry dock.

Landfall Restaurant, 412 Water St, Point Hudson, 360/385-5814 Waterfront, breakfast, lunch, dinner. Seafood, omelettes, BBQ's and homemade burgers and desserts.

Lanza's Ristorante, 1020 Lawrence Street, 360/379-1900 Voted best pasta in PT. Uptown, live music.

Lonny's Restaurant , 2330 Washington Street (Boat Haven), 360/385-0700 PT votes it best gourmet food and most romantic. Mediterranean bistro. *lonnys.com*

Manresa Castle, 7th & Sheridan Streets, 360/385-5750 Four star menu, Victorian elegance *manresacastle.com*

Maxwell's Brewery & Pub, 126 Quincy Street, (Old Town Tavern) 360/379-6438 Serves its own brews, seafood menu, waterfront.

The Original Oyster House, Hwy 101, west of Hwy 20, 360/385-1785 Out of town on Discovery Bay with Dabob Bay oysters, seafood, steaks, poultry.

Osamu Ocean Grill & Sushi Bar, 1208 Water Street, 360/379-4000 Japanese sushi and nouvelle cuisine. *OsamuOceanGrill.com*

Otter Crossing Cafe, 130 Hudson St., Point Hudson, 360/379-0592 Breakfast, lunch on the Point Hudson waterfront. *Ottercrossing.com*

Plaza Soda Fountain, 1151 Water St. (in Don's Pharmacy), 360/385-2622 Old-time ice cream sundaes, shakes, homemade bread pudding and pies. Homemade soups and daily specials.

The Public House, 1038 Water Street, 360/385-9708 Microbrews, pub lunches & dinners, desserts, live entertainment. *dreamcitycatering.com*

Salal Cafe, 634 Water Street, 360/385-653 Voted best breakfast in PT for 5 years. Also serving lunches, dinners and desserts

Sentosa, 218 Polk Street, 360/385-2378 Japanese sushi, noodle dishes.

Shanghai, 265 Point Hudson, 360/385-4810 Providing classic Chinese cuisine for 15 years, waterfront view.

Silverwater Cafe, 237 Taylor Street, 360/385-6448 Locals vote Silverwater Cafe the best seafood and the best soup. Pacific Northwest cuisine.

The Upstage, 923 Washington Street, 360/385-2216 Organic Northwest and Mediterranean cuisine, Indian food on Thursdays, seafood, steak, salads and pizzas. Entertainment.

Uptown Pub, 1016 Lawrence St, 360/385-1530 Micro brews, wines, pub grub and local entertainment.

Waterfront Pizza, 951 Water Street, 360/385-6629 Rated best pizza in town

Wild Coho, 1044 Lawrence Street, 360/379-1030 Uptown bistro, award winning chef buys from local bakeries, fishermen and organic growers. *thewildcoho.com*

Poulsbo

Azteca, 19045 St Hwy 305, 360/779-7427 Mexican

Farm Kitchen, 24309 Port Gamble Rd NE, 360/297-6615, Saturday morning farm breakfasts, *farmkitchen.com*

Golden Lion, 19438 E 7th at Poulsbo Village, 360/697-5066 Chinese Szechuan, Mandarin & Cantonese. Dine in/carry out.

Los Cabos Grill, 18751 St Hwy 305, 360/779-1445 Mexican

Mitzel's American Kitchen, 760 NE Liberty Rd (Poulsbo Village), 360/697-2215. Family dining

Vege Restaurant, 18713 St Hwy 305, 360/697-2538 SE Asian vegetarian.

Quilcene

Loggers Landing, Hwy 101, 360/765-3161

The Whistling Oyster, Hwy 101, 360/765-9508

Seabeck

Barbie's Seabeck Bay Cafe, 15384 Seabeck Hwy NW, 360/830-5532 Breakfast to 5 pm

Seabeck Pizza, 15376 Seabeck Hwy N, 360/830-4839 Pizza

Willcox House, 2390 Tekiu Road NW, 360/830-4492, Regional cuisine with international touches, *willcoxhouse.com*

Sequim

Chinese Gardens, 271 S 7th Av, 360/683-4525 Chinese

Dupuis Restaurant, Hwy 101 between Sequim & Pt Angeles, 360/457-8033, Steak & seafood *dupuisrestaurant.com*

El Cazador, 531 W Washington St, 360/683-4788 Mexican, American

Elements Cafe, 126 E Washington St, 360/681-5060 Continental Cafe breakfast & lunch

Greenside Grill, 1965 Woodcock Rd, 360/683-3331 Steaks, seafood *dungenessgolf.com*

Gwennie's, 701 E. Washington St, 360/683-4157 Homestyle

Khu Larb Thai, 120 W. Bell, 360/ 681-8550, Thai

Las Palomas, 1085 E. Washington, 360/681-3842 Mexican, American

Marina Restaurant, 2577 W Sequim Bay Rd, 360/681-0577 northolympic.com/marina

Oak Table, 292 W. Bell St, 360/683-2179 Gourmet breakfasts

Petals Garden Cafe at Cedarbrook Herb Farm, 1345 S Sequim Ave, 360/683-4541 Gourmet cafe. *petalscafe.com*

Tarcisio's The Italian Place, 609 W. Washington St 360/683-5809

Three Crabs, 101 Three Crabs Rd, 360/683-4264 Seafood specialties

Shelton

Aguila Express, 2126 Olympic Highway North, Mountain View.360/432-7830. Homemade burritos, Mexican specialties

Big E Bar and Grill, 324 W Railroad Av, 360/426-2186. Bar with full-service restaurant.

Capital Family Diner, 116 W Railroad Av, 360/432-2777 Full-service restaurant.

Hattie Rose Cafe, 405 W Railroad Av, 360/426-4113 Creative cuisine, weekday lunches, monthly dinners

Lake Nahwatzel Resort, 12900 W. Shelton-Matlock Rd, 360/426-8323 American cuisine and prime rib on weekends.

Las Palmas, 116 East Cota Street, 360/432-3220 Authentic Mexican taqueria.

Legends, 91 W. State Route 108 (In Little Creek Casino just west of Highway 101 at the Kamilche Rd exit), 360/427-7711 Buffet.

Pine Tree Restaurant, 102 S First St, 360/426-2604 Full-service restaurant

Royal Shanghai Restaurant and Lounge, 2517 Olympic Hwy N, Mountain View, 360/427-0560. Chinese-American buffet

Steven's Fine Dining, 204 W Railroad Av, 360/426-4407 Northwest cuisine.

Travaglione's, 825 W. Franklin, 360/427-3844 Italian food.

Xinh's Clam & Oyster House, 221 W Railroad Av, 360/427-8709 Gourmet seafood dishes with SE Asian influence.

Silverdale

Alladin's Palace, 9399 Ridgetop Blvd, 360/698-6599 Mediterranean

Bahn Thai, 9811 Mickelberry Rd, 360/698-3663 Thai

Elsie's Restaurant, 10424 Silverdale Way Nw, 360/692-2649

Gandhi Indian Cuisine, 9621 Mickelberry Rd Suite 101, 360/662-0599, East Indian cuisine

Golden Grill Mongolian Barbeque, 9469 Silverdale Way NW, 360/692-5504

Hakata, 10876 Myhre Pl, 360/698-0929 Japanese

Kings Wok Buffet, 9960 Silverdale Way Nw, 360/337-2512 Chinese buffet

Mariner Grill at Red Lion Hotel, 3073 NW Bucklin Hill Rd, 360/692-0748 Casual dining

Osaka, 10408 Silverdale Way NW, 360/698-7266 Japanese

Silver City Restaurant & Brewery 2799 NW Myhre RD, 360/698-5879 Steak, seafood, specialties

Waterfront Park Bakery & Cafe, 3472 Nw Byron St, 360/698-2991

Yacht Club Broiler, 9226 Bayshore Dr, 360/698-1601 Seafood, steak

Sol Duc

Sol Duc Hot Springs Restaurant (Seasonal), (35 mi NE of Forks on Sol Duc Hot Springs Rd), 360/327-3583, Breakfast, lunch and dinner, Beer & Wine

Suquamish

Clearwater Casino, Agate Pass Bridge, 360/598-6889, *clearwatercasino.com*

Sea View Chinese Restaurant, 7220 NE Parkway, 360/598-3955

Bella Luna Pizzeria, 18471 Augusta Av NE, 360/598-5398

Union

Alderbrook Inn, 7101 E Hwy 106, 360/898-2200 Fine dining.

Victoria's, 6790 E Hwy 106, 360/898-4400. Northwest cuisine using seasonal organic local ingredients in the original "Sherwood Forest Dining Room".

Union Bay Cafe, 5121 E Hwy 106, 360/898-2462

Vashon Island

Casa Bonita Mexican Restaurant, 17623 100th Av SW, 206/463-6452

Fred's Homegrown Restaurant & Deli, 17614 Vashon Hwy Sw, 206/463-6302 Using locally grown vegetables and fruits.

Mary Martha's Good Things to Eat, Thriftway Plaza, 206/463-3720 Bakery, sandwiches

The Rock Island Pub and Pizza, 17322 Vashon Hwy SW, 206/463-6813 Gourmet hand tossed pizzas and salads. *therockisland.com*

Stray Dog Cafe, 17530 Vashon Hwy SW, 206/463-7833

Westport

Barbara's By the Sea, 2323 Westhaven Dr, 360/268-1329 Local seafood, homemade desserts

Cowboy Bob's, 2581 Westhaven, 360/268-9228 Prime Rib, steak, seafood, BBQ. Ocean & mountain views.

Islander, 4212 Corner of Westhaven & Neddie Roes Dr, 360/268-9166,800/322-1740, Fresh Seafood and Steak, *westportislander.com*

Las Maracas #3, 202 W. Ocean Av, 360/268-6272, Authentic Mexican food

Sourdough Lil's, 301 Dock Street, 360/268-9700 Fish & chips; chowder, great seafood. Casual.

LODGING

If you would rather not be surprised (and possibly also thereby delighted) you will find the usual national lodging chains well-represented in Bremerton, Poulsbo, Silverdale, Sequim, Port Angeles, and Aberdeen/Hoqiam.

As innkeepers we prefer in this publication, whenever possible, to celebrate locally-owned establishments that offer more creative and personal experiences.

This list is not all-inclusive, and we have not personally visited or stayed at all of these establishments. Also, this information may go out of date sooner than we can print a new edition of this book.

Please check with the local chamber of commerce/ visitor information center (or their web site) for the most comprehensive and up-to-date listings and recommendations.

And naturally we are going to shine the spotlight extra brightly on all the members of our Bainbridge Island Lodging Association.

Aberdeen
Aberdeen Mansion Inn, 807 North "M" St 888/533-7079, 360/533-7079, *aberdeenmansion.com*

A Harbor View Bed and Breakfast, 113 West 11th St, 877/868-6273, 360/533-7996, *aharborview.com*

Hoquiam's Castle Bed and Breakfast, 515 Chenault Av, 360/533-2005, *hoquiamscastle.com*

Bainbridge Island
Arrow Point Guest House, 10159 Arrow Pt Dr, 206/842-0967, *arrowpointguesthouse.com*

Aunt Margie's Beach, 6670 Bayview Blvd, 206/842-6969. *bicomnet.com/margies*

Bainbridge House, 206/842-1599, *bainbridgehouse.com*

Bainbridge Island Beach Cottage, 206/999-9655, *bainbridgebeachcottage.com*

Baker Hill B&B, 4502 Sorrel AV NE, *206/855.9721, bakerhillbedandbreakfast.com*

Blackberry Hill Farm Bicycle Inn, 206/842-9024, *bainbridgelodging.com/blackberryhill*

Buchanan Inn, 8494 NE Oddfellows Rd, 800/598-3926 or 206/780-9258, *buchananinn.com*

Captain's House, 234 Parfitt Way, 206/842-3557, *bainbridgelodging.com/captainshouse*

Cedar Meadows, 10411 NE Old Creosote Hill Rd, 206/842-5291, *Bainbridgelodging.com/cedarmeadows*

Eagle Harbor Inn, 291 Madison Av S, 206/842-1446. *theeagleharborinn.com*

Fuurin-Oka Futon & Breakfast, 12580 Vista Dr NE, 206/842-4916, *futonandbreakfast.com*

Holly Lane Gardens, 9432 Holly Farm Ln, 206/842-8959, *bainbridgelodging.com/hollylane*

Island Country Inn & Suites, 920 Hildebrand Ln, 800/842-8429 or 206/842-8429, *nwcountryinns.com*

Janelle Place, 641 Janelle Place, 206/780-2643, *janelleplace.com*

Kellerman Creek B&B, 10220 NE Roberts Rd, 206/855-8081, *kellermancreek.com*

Log House at Frog Rock Lavender Farm, 14414 Madison Av N, 206/780-5368, *frogrocklavender.com*

Our Country Haus, 13718 Ellingsen Rd, 206/842-8425, *ourcountryhaus.com*

Port Madison Carriage House, 15113 Washington Av 206/842-4472, *portmadisoncarriagehouse.com*

Rolling Bay House, 11475 Kallgren Rd, 206/780-1532, *bainbridgelodging.com/rollingbay*

Saxon Cottage, 13671 Madison Av, 206/842-0382, *saxoncot.com*

Seabold Cottage, 14125 Henderson Rd, 206/780-2128, *seaboldcottage.com*

Seattle View Bed & Breakfast, 206/855-0979, *seattleviewbandb.com*

Skiff Point Guest House, Skiff Point, 206/842-7026, *skiffpoint.com*

SpringRidge Gardens, 7686 Springridge Rd NE, 206/842-7369, *SpringRidgeGardens.com*

The Studio, 243A Lovell Ave SW, 206/842-1599, *bainbridgelodging.com/thestudio*

Twin Rose Guest House, 206/842-1599, *bainbridgehouse.com*

Waterfall Gardens Private Suites, 7269 NE Bergman Rd, 206/842-1434, *waterfall-gardens.com*

Willow Brook Farm Cottage, 12600 Miller Rd NE, 206/842-8034, *willowbrookfarm.com*

Wing Point Cottage Apartment, 206/855/1171 or 206/780-0458, *bainbridgelodging.com/wingpoint*

Belfair
Cady Lake Manor, 360/372-2673, cadylake.com

Selah Inn, 130 NE Dulalip landing, 877/232-7941, 360/275-0916, *selahinn.com*

Bremerton
Highland Cottage B & B, 622 Highland Ave, 360/373-2235

Illahee Manor Bed & Breakfast, 6680 Illahee Rd NE, 800/693-6680, 360/698-75555, *comstation.com/illaheemanor*

Brinnon
Brinnon Flats Bed and Breakfast, 360/796-4935, *brinnonflats.com*

Cabin on the Canal, 111 Cedar Cove Rd, 206/782-3868, *cabinonthecanal.com*

Elk Meadows Bed and Breakfast, 3485 Dosewallips Rd, 360/796-4886, *elkmeadowswa.com*

Clallam Bay
Chito Beach Resort, 7639 Hwy 112, 360/963-2581, *chitobeach.com*

Lost Resort at Lake Ozette, 20860 Hoko-Ozette Rd, 800/950-2899, 360/963-2899, *northolympic.com/lostresort*

Elma
Abel House Bed & Breakfast, 117 Fleet St S, Montesano, WA 98563, 360/249-6002, *ablehouse.com*

Grays Harbor Hostel/Guest House, 6 Ginny Lane, Elma, Washington, 98541; 360/482-3119; 360/482-4053

Forks
Bear Creek Homestead B&B, 800/485-1721, 360/327-3699, *bearcreekhomestead.com*

Brightwater House B&B, 440 Brightwater Dr, 360/374-5453, *brightwaterhouse.com*

Dew Drop Inn, 100 Fernhill Rd, 888/433-9376, 360/374-4055, *dewdropinnmotel.com*

Eagle Point Inn B&B, 384 Storman Norman Ln, 360/327-3236, *eaglepointinn.com*

Huckleberry Lodge B&B, 1171 Big Pine Wy, 888/822-6008, 360/ 374-6008, *huckleberrylodge.com*

Manitou Lodge B&B, 813 Kilmer Rd, 360/374-6295, *manitoulodge.com*

Miller Tree Inn B&B, 654 E Division St, 800-943-6563, 360/374-6806, *millertreeinn.com*

Misty Valley Inn B&B, 194894 Hwy 101 N, 877/374-9389, 360/374-9389, *mistyvalleyinn.com*

Mountain View Cabin Resort, 285 Maxfield Homestead Rd, 360/374-6486,

River Inn B&B, 2596 Bogachiel Wy, 360/374-6526

Rain Forest Hostel, 169312 Hwy 101, 360/374-2270, *rainforesthostel.com*

Shadynook Cottage B&B, 81 Ash Av, 360/374-5497, *shadynookcottage.com*

Three Rivers B&B, 7563 La Push Rd, 360/374-2228, *threeriversbandb.com*

Gig Harbor

Aloha Beachside B&B, 8318 State Route 302, Purdy; 1-888/ALOHA-BB, *alohabeachsidebb.com*

Beachside B&B, 679 Kamus Dr, Fox Island, 253/594-2524, *beachsidebb.com*

Cady Lake Manor B&B, 1471 NE DeWatto Rd, Tahuya; 360/372-2673, *cadylake.com*

Child's House B&B, 8331 SE Willock Rd, Ollala, 253/857-4252

The Fountains B&B, 926 120th St, Gig Harbor, 253/851-6262, *fountainsbb.com*

Harborside B&B; 8708 Goodman Dr, Gig Harbor, 253/851-1795

Island Escape B&B, 210 Island Blvd, Fox Island, 253/594-2044, *island-escape.com*

No Cabbages B&B, 7712 Goodman Dr NW, 253/858-7797, *gigharbor.com/nocabbages*

Olde Glencove Hotel, 253/884-2835, *glencovehotel.com*

Peacock Hill Guest House, 9520 Peacock Hill Av, 253/858-3322, *virtualcities.com/wa/peacock.htm*

Point View B&B; 2407 56th St NW, Gig Harbor, 253/851-5768

The Rose of Gig Harbor, 3202 Harborview Dr, Gig Harbor, 253/853-7990, Toll Free: 877-640-ROSE (7673) *gigharborrose.com*

Rosedale B&B, Ray Nash D, Gig Harbor, 253/851-5420, *rosedalebnb.com*

Rosegate B&B, 9409 86th Av NW, Gig Harbor, 253/851-3179, *rosegatebb.com*

Still Waters B&B; 13202 Olympic Dr. SE, Olalla, 253/857-5111

Waterfront Inn, 9017 N. Harborview Dr, 253/857-0770, *waterfront-inn.com*

The Waters Edge B&B, 8610 Goodman Dr, NW, 253/851-3890, *thewatersedgebb.com*

Westbay Guest Cottage, 2515 48th Av NW, 800/420-3033 or 253/265-3033, *westbaycottage.com*

Grayland

The Beach House, State Rte 105, 888/822-8110, 509/235-8110

Bishop Guest Suites, 714 Washington St, 800/824-4738, *waypt.com/bishop*

Fantasy Cabins by Simmodd, 1624 State Rte 105, 888/652-4666 or 360/267-3234

Ocean Gate Resort, 1939 State Rt. 105 S, PO Box 67, 360/267-1956,800/473-1956

Simmodd Fantasy Cabins, P O Box 631, 1624 State Route 105, 888/652-4666 or 360/267-3234 Theme getaway cabins that provide an escape from reality! Jungle/Treehouse; Rustic 2-Story; Goldilocks, *fantasycabins.net*

Tokeland Hotel & Restaurant, 100 Hotel Rd, Tokeland, 360/267-7006 *tokelandhotel.com*

Hansville

Guest House at Twin Spits, 2570 Twin Spits Rd, 360/638-1001

Hoh

Hoh Humm Ranch B&B, 171763 Hwy 101, 360/374-5337, *olypen.com/hohhumm*

Hoh River Resort, 175443 Hwy 101, 360/374-5566

Hoodsport

Glen Ayr Canal Resort, 800/367-9522 or 360/877-9522 *hoodsportwa.com/Glen-Ayr*

Lake Cushman Resort, 360/877-9630
lakecushman.com

Lilliwaup Store & Motel, 360/877-0001

Mike's Beach Resort RV Park, Marina & Dive Center, 800/231-5324

Minerva Beach Resort, 866/500-5145, 360/877-5145

Rest-A-While RV Park, Marina & Dive Center, 360/877-9474

Sunrise Resort & Motel, 360/877-9474

Hoquiam

Hoquiam's Castle Bed and Breakfast, 515 Chenault Ave, 360/533-2005, *hoquiamscastle.com*

Kalaloch

Kalaloch Lodge, 157151 Hwy 101, 360/962-2271, *visitkalaloch.com*

Keyport

FoxBrier Cottage, (360) 779-7263, *bainbridgelodging.com/foxbrier*

Kingston

Kingston House Bed & Breakfast, 26117 Ohio Av Ne, 360/297/8818. *kingstonhousebb.com*

Lake Crescent

Lake Crescent Lodge, 416 Lake Crescent Rd, 360/928-3211, *lakecrescentlodge.com*

Log Cabin Resort, 3183 East Beach Rd, 360/928-3325, *logcabinresort.net*

Lake Quinault

Lake Quinault Lodge, 345 South Shore Rd, 800/562-6672, 360/288-2900, *visitlakequinault.com*

Lake Quinault Rain Forest Resort Village, 516 South Shore Rd, 800/255-6936, 360/288-2535, *rainforestresort.com*

Lake Quinault Resort, 314 North Shore Rd, 800/650-2362, 360/288-2362, *lakequinault.com*

La Push

La Push Ocean Park Resort, 770 Main St, 800/487-12667, 360/374-5267, *ocean-park.org*

Marrowstone Island

Beach Cottages on Marrowstone, 10 Beach Drive, Nordland, 360/385-3077, 800/871-3077 *beachcottagegetaway.com*

Fort Flagler Hostel, 10621 Flagler Road, Nordland, 360/385-1288

Honey Moon Cabin, 360/385-4644, *marrowstone.com/honeymooncabin/*

Neah Bay

Cape Motel & RV Park, 1500 Bayview Av, 360/645-2250

Silver Salmon Resort & RV Park, Bayview Av, 888/713-6477, 360/645-2388, silversalmonresort.com

Snow Creek Resort, Hwy 112, 800/883-1464, 360/645-2284

Tyee Motel, Bayview Av, 360/645-2223

North Beach

Iron Springs Ocean Beach Resort, PO Box 207, Copalis Beach, WA 98535, 360/276-4230, *ironspringsresort.com*

Tidelands Resort, 2991 SR 109 North, P.O. Box 36, Copalis Beach, WA 98535, *tidelandsresort.com*

Hi-Tide Ocean Beach Resort, Moclips, 360/276-4142, *hi-tide-resort.com*

Ocean Crest Resort, Moclips, 800/684-8439, 360/276-4465, *oceancrestresort.com*

Vacation Getaway, The, 2578 SR 109 Ocean City, WA 98569, 360/289-5840, *wa-accommodations.com/nw/vacationgetaway*

Beach Avenue Bed & Breakfast, P. O. Box 284, Pacific Beach, WA 98571, 360/276-4727 *pacificbeachwa.com/lodging/babb/beachave.html*

Pacific Beach Inn, 12 First St S, Pacific Beach, WA 98571, 360/276-4433, 360/276-4433, *pbinn.com*

Sand Dollar Inn, PO Box 206, Pacific Beach, WA 98571, 360/276-4525, *sanddollarinn.net*

Sandpiper Beach Resort, P.O. Box A, Pacific Beach, WA 98571, 800/56-PIPER *sandpiper-resort.com*

Ocean Shores

Caroline Inn, 888/70-BEACH, *oceanshores.com/romantic_getaways/*

Gibson's Bed & Breakfast, The, 125 Taholah St NE, 360/289-7960, *thegibsonsbandb.com*

Judith Ann Inn, 888/70-BEACH, *oceanshores.com/romantic_getaways/*

Ocean Shores, WA 98569, *silverwavesbandb.com/*

Ocean Shores, WA 98569 360/289-7960 thegibsonsbandb.com/

Silverwaves Bed & Breakfast, 888/257-0894, 360/289-2490, 982 Point Brown Av

Port Angeles

BJ's Garden Gate Bed & Breakfast, 397 Monterra Dr, 360/452-2322, 800/880-1332, *bjgarden.com*

Best Western Olympic Lodge, 360/452-2993, 800/600-2993, *portangeleshotelmotel.com*

Elwha Ranch, 905 Herrick Rd, 360/457-6540, *northolympic.com/elwharanch*

Foxglove Bed and Breakfast, 131 E12th Street, 360/417-1277, *foxglovebandb.com*

Clarks' Harbor View, 1426 W 4th St, 360/457-9891, *bbchannel.com/bbc/p215392.asp*

Red Lion Hotel Port Angeles, 360/452-9215, 800/RED-LION, *redlion.com*

The Tudor Inn, 1108 S. Oak St, 360/ 452-3138, *tudorinn.com*

A Hidden Haven & Water Garden Cottages, 1428 Dan Kelly Rd, 877/418-0938, 360/452-2719, *ahiddenhaven.com*

Sol Duc River Lodge B&B, 206114 Hwy 101N, 866/868-0128, 360/327-3709, i

Sol Duc Hot Springs Resort, Sol Duc River Rd, 360/327-3583, northolympic.com/solduc

Port Orchard

Guesthouse Inn, 220 Bravo Terrace, 360/895-7818

Northwest Interlude B&B, 3377 Sarann Ave E, 360/871-4676

Reflections Bed & Breakfast, 3878 Reflection Lane E, 360/ 871-5582, *portorchard.com/reflections/*

Port Townsend

Annapurna Inn & Spa, 538 Adams St, 800/868-2662, *annapurnaretreat-spa.com*

Bishop Guest Suites, 714 Washington St, 800/824-4738, *waypt.com/bishop*

Captain John Quincy Adams House, 1028 Tyler St, 888/385-1258, *captnjqadams.com*

Chanticleer Inn, 1208 Franklin St, 800/858-9421, *chanticleerbb.com*

Commander's Beach House, 400 Hudson St, 888/385-1778, *commandersbeachhouse.com*

Baker House, 800/240-0725,

Blue Gull Inn, 1310 Clay St, 888/700-0205, *bluegullinn.com*

English Inn, 718 F Street, 800/254-5302, *english-inn.com*

Holly Hill House, 611 Polk St, 800/435-1454, *hollyhillhouse.com*

James House, 1238 Washington St, 800/385-1238, *jameshouse.com*

Old Consulate Inn, 313 Walker at Washington, 800/300-6753, *oldconsulateinn.com*

Quimper Inn, 1306 Franklin St, 800/557-1060, *olympus.net/quimper*

Ravenscroft Inn, 533 Quincy St, 800/782-2691, *ravenscroftinn.com*

Poulsbo

Brauer Cove Guest House, 16709 Brauer Rd, 360/779-4153, *brauercove.com*

Farm Kitchen Guest House, 24309 Port Gamble Rd NE, 360/297-6615, *farmkitchen.com*

Foxbridge B&B, 30680 Hwy 3 NE, 360/598-5599, *foxbridge.com*

Libery Place Guest House, 17030 Lemolo Shore Dr NE, 360/779-4943, *libertybayguesthouse.com*

Manor Farm Inn, 26069 Big Valley Rd, 360/779-4628, *manorfarminn.com*

Murphy House B&B, 19083 Front St, 800/779-1606, 360-779-1606, *murphyhousebnb.com*

Quilcene

Mount Walker Inn, Hwy 101, 360/765-3410, *mountwalkerinn.com*

Quilcene Hotel, 11 Quilcene Av, 360/765-3868, *quilcenehotel.com*

Seabeck

Willcox House Country Inn, 2390 Tekiu Rd NW, 800/725-9477, 360/830-4492, *willcoxhouse.com*

Sekiu

Bay Motel, 15562 Hwy 112, 360/963-2444, northolympic.com/baymotel

Curley's Resort & Dive Center, 291 Front Street, 800/542-9680, 360/963-2281, *curleyresort.com*

Herb's Motel & Charters, 411 Front St, 360/963-2346, *herbsmotel.com*

King Fisher Inn B&B, 1562 Hwy 112,,888/622-8216, 360/645-2150, *kingfisherenterprises.com*

Olson's Resort, 444 Front St, 360/963-2311, *norholympic.com/olsons*

Straitside Resort, 241 Front St, 360/963-2100, *olypen.com/strait*

Van Riper's Resort, 280 Front St, 360/963-2334, *olypen.com/vanrip*

Sequim

Bearheart Inn Bed & Breakfast, 1290 Gardiner Beach Rd, 360/797-7500, *bearheartinn.com*

Domaine Madeleine, 146 Wildflower Lane, 360/457-4174, *domainmadeleine.com*

Dungeness Lodge, 1330 Jamestown Rd, 877/294-0173, 360/582-0181, *dungenesslodge.com*

The Greywolf Inn, 395 Keeler Rd, 360/683-5889, 800/914-WOLF, *greywolfinn.com*

Helga's Edelweiss B&B, 235 Roberson Rd, 360/681-2873, *angelfire.com/wa2/edelweiss*

Toad Hall Bed and Breakfast, 12 Jesslyn Lane/Sequim Ave, 360/681-2534, *toadhallbandb.com*

Shelton

Rest Full Farm B&B, W 2230 Shelton Valley Rd, 360/426-8774

Shelton Inn Motel, 628 W Railroad Ave, 360/426-4468

Twin River Ranch Bed & BreakfastE5730 State Rt 3, (360) 426-1023

Silverdale

Seaside Manor Bed & Breakfast, Silverdale, WA 98383, 360/308-8274

Seabreeze Beach Cottage and Spa, 16609 Olympic View Rd NW, 360/692-4648

Tracyton Waterfront Manor, 6425 Tracyton Blvd Tracyton, 360/405-1308, 360/981-5691

Suquamish

Agate Beach Guest House, 17230 Angeline Av S, 360/598-4086, *guesthouse-agatebeach.com*

The Beach House, 17922 Angeline Avenue South 330/779-7093, *thebeachbb.com*

Union

Old Hatchery Lake B&B, 231 E Old Hatchery Lane, 360/898-5253, *oldhatcherylake.com*

Vashon Island

All Seasons Waterfront, 12817 SW Bachelor Road 206/463-3498, *allseasonswaterfront.com*

Angels of the Sea B&B, 26431 99th Av SW, 800/798-9249, 206/463-6980, *angelsofthesea.com*

Artist's Studio Loft B&B, 16529 91st Av SW, 206/463-2583, *asl-bnb.com*

AYH International Hostel, 12119 SW Cove Rd, 206/ 463-2592, *vashonhostel.com* Sleep in covered wagons, Indian teepees or cozy private rooms. Open May1-Oct. 31, lodge year round

Betty MacDonald Farm Cottage, 12000 99th Av SW 1-888-EATNSLEEP, 206/567-4227, bettymacdonaldfarm.com

Boulder Lodge, 80th Lane, Ellisport location, 206/567-0999

Castle Hill B&B, 26734 94th Av SW, 206/463-5491

Lavender Duck, 16503 Vashon Hwy SW, 206/463-2592, *vashonhostel.com*

Northview Guest House, 206/463-9181, *onvashon.com*

Paradise Valley Farm, 21831 107th SW, 206/463-9815

Sea Lotus Day Spa and B&B, 206/567-5565

Sojourn House, 18211 Vashon Hwy SW, 206/ 463-5437, 463-5193, *sojournhouse.net*

Steen Estate B&B, 10924 SW Cove Rd, 206/463-7763, *steenestate.com*

Sunset Beach Paradise, 206/325-3067, 567-5295 *sunsetbeachparadise.com*

Swallow's Nest Guest Cottages, 6030 SW 248th St, 800/ANYNEST, 206/ 463-2646, *vashonislandcottages.com*

Twinbrooks Lodge Retreat Center, P.O. Box 1931 Vashon, WA 98070, 206/463-1888 / Fax: 206/ 463-1898

Van Gelder's Retreat, PO Box 1328, 18522 Beall Rd SW, Vashon, WA 98070, 206/463-3684

Westport

Chateau Westport, 710 West Hancock, 800/255-9101, 360/268-9101

Frank L Aquatic Garden Resort, 725 S Montesano, 360/268-9200

Harbor Resort, 871 Neddie Rose Dr, 360/268-0169, *harborresort.com*

Ocean Avenue Inn, 275 Ocean Av, 888/692-5262, 360/ 268-9278

Seagull's Nest Motel, 830 N Montesano, 888/613-9078, 360/268-9711

PUBLIC CAMPGROUNDS

Here is a list of the most popular public campground facililties, organized by jurisdiction . More information is available at their web sites.

There are many more camping options at private campgrounds and RV parks. Local chambers of commerce can provide details.

Olympic National Park Campgrounds   www.nps.gov/olym

No reservations. Information: 360/565-3130 (No RV hookups, showers, laundry)

Campground	# Sites	Tent	RV	Year Round	Rest Rooms	Drinking Water	RV Dump
Altaire Elwha River Valley	30	●	●		●	●	
Deer Park Deer Park	14	●			●	●	
Elwha Elwha River Valley	40	●	●	●	●	●	
Fairholm Lake Crescent	88	●	●		●	●	●
Graves Creek Lake Quinault	30	●	●		●	●	
Heart of the Hills Port Angeles, Hurricane Ridge	105	●	●	●	●	●	
Hoh Hoh River Valley	88	●	●	●	●	●	●
Kalaloch Kalaloch	175	●	●	●	●	●	●
Mora La Push	94	●	●		●	●	●
Ozette Neah Bay	13	●	●	●	●	●	
Sol Duc Sol Duc River	80	●	●		●	●	●
Staircase Lake Cushman	56	●	●	●	●	●	

Washington State Park Campgrounds   www.parks.wa.gov

Campground	# Sites	RV Hookups	Tent	RV	Year Round	Rest Rooms	Drinking Water	RV Dump
Fay-Bainbridge	36		●	●		●	●	●
Bainbridge Island 800/233-0321	No reservations							
Kitsap Memorial	51		●	●	●	●	●	●
Port Gamble 800/233-0321	No reservations							
Scenic Beach	50		●	●		●	●	●
Seabeck 800/233-0321	Reservations							
Fort Flagler 800/452-5687	102	14	●	●		●	●	●
Marrowstone Island/Port Hadlock	Reservations							
Fort Worden	80	30	●	●	●	●	●	●
Port Townsend 360/385-4730	Reservations							
Old Fort Townsend	43		●	●		●	●	
Port Townsend 360/233-0321	No reservations							
Dosewallips	88	40	●	●	●	●	●	●
Brinnon 800/233-0321	Reservations							
Sequim Bay	60	26	●	●	●	●	●	●
Sequim 800/233-0321	Reservations							
Potlatch	37	18	●	●		●	●	●
Hoodsport 800/233-0321	No reservations							
Twanoh	26	9	●	●		●	●	●
Union 800/233-0321	No reservations							
Belfair	137	47	●	●	●	●	●	●
Belfair 800/452-5687	Reservations							
Bogachiel	36	6	●	●	●	●	●	●
Forks 800/233-0321	No reservations							
Pacific Beach	64		●	●	●	●	●	●
Pacific Beach 800/452-5687	Reservations							
Ocean City	149	29	●	●	●	●	●	●
Ocean City 800/452-5687	Reservations							
Twin Harbors	249	49	●	●		●	●	●
Westport 800/452-5687	Reservations							
Grayland Beach	60	60	●	●	●	●	●	
Grayland 800/452-5687	Reservations							
Lake Sylvia	35		●	●	●	●		●
Montesano 800/233-0321	No reservations							
Schafer	47	6	●	●		●	●	●
Montesano 800/233-0321	No reservations							
Jarrell Cove	20		●	●		●	●	
Shelton 800/233-0321	Reservations							

Olympic National Forest Campgrounds www.fs.fed.us/r6/olympic/recreation/cmpgrds.html

No reservations. (No RV hookups, showers, laundry)

Campground	# Sites	Tent	RV	Year Round	Rest Rooms	Drinking Water	RV Dump
Big Creek Lake Cushman 360/877-5254	23	●	●		●	●	
Brown Creek Shelton 360/877-5254	20	●	●	●	●	●	
Coho Wynoochee Valley 360/877-5254	56	●	●		●	●	●
Collins Duckabush River 360/877-5254	16	●	●		●	●	
Elkhorn Dosewallips River 360/765-3368	20	●	●		●	●	
Falls Creek Lake Quinault 360/288-2525	31	●	●		●	●	
Falls View Quilcene 360/765-3368	14	●	●		●	●	
Hamma Hamma Hamma Hamma River 360/877-5254	15	●	●		●	●	
Klahowya Sol Duc River 360/374-6522	55	●	●		●	●	
Lena Creek Hoodsport 360/877-5254	13	●	●		●	●	
Seal Rock Brinnon 360/765-3368	41	●	●		●	●	
Willaby Lake Quinault 360/288-2525	22	●	●		●	●	

PLACES TO CYCLE

Bainbridge Island

Chilly Hilly Loop
Battle Point Park
Gazzam Lake MB

Belfair

Tahuya Loop MB

Hood Canal

Toandos Peninsula Loop

Kalaloch

Kalaloch-Clearwater Loop

Kingston

Kingston-Hansville Loop
Mosquito Fleet Trail - Kingston to Southworth

Lake Crescent

Spruce Railroad Trail

Lake Quinault

Lake Quinault Loop

Port Angeles

PA to Sol Duc Hot Springs
Olympic Discovery Trail -- PA-Sequim
Foothills Trail MB

Port Gamble

North Kitsap Loop
Pope Resources Recreational Area MB

Port Orchard

PO to Southworth
Banner Forest MB

Port Townsend

PT Loop
Marrowstone Island

Quilcene

Quilcene Range Ride

Seabeck

Gold Creek Trail to Green Mountain MB
Wildcat Lake Trail MB

Sequim

Scenic Loop
Gold Creek Loop MB
Olympic Discovery Trail Sequim-Port Angeles

Shelton

Shelton-Union Loop
Shelton-Satsop Loop

Vashon Island

Vashon Island Loop

FAVORITE BIRDWATCHING AREAS

Western Washington is an important flyway in the migration routes of many species. We also have our share of year-round residents – some native, some imported. One of the advantages of the West Sound area is the variety of habitats in close proximity to each other. In some localities you can go from seashore to marshland to conifer forest to above-the-treeline mountain areas in a very short time.

Aberdeen
Lake Swano Nature Trails
John's River Wildlife Area

Bainbridge Island
Kane Cemetery, Port Madison heron rookery
Peterson Hill Road heron rookery
Bloedel Reserve
Battle Point Park
Fay-Bainbridge State Park
Point Monroe lagoon
Fort Ward State Park
Port Blakely Waterfront Park
Winslow Waterfront Park
Meigs Farm Park
Gazzam Lake

Belfair
Theler Wetlands
Belfair State Park
Twanoh State Park

Brinnon
Dosewallips Estuary
Dosewallips State Park
Pleasant Harbor
Duckabush Estuary

Chimacum
Oak Bay County Park

Clallam Bay/Sekiu
Clallam Bay County Park

Sekiu River mouth
Seal and Sail Rocks

Elma/Satsop
Chehalis Wildlife Area

Forks
Bogachiel State Park

Grayland
Grayland Beach State Park
Midway Beach Road

Hansville
Point No Point Lighthouse area
Point No Point County Park
Bucks Lake
Foulweather Bluff Nature Conservancy Preserve
Twinspits sandspit

Hood Canal
Hood Canal Bridge
Shine Tidelands State Park
Triton Cove State Park

Hoodsport
Lake Cushman area
Hamma Hamma Estuary
Potlatch State Park

Hoh Rain Forest
Visitor Center
Hoh Campground

Hall of Mosses Trail
Spruce Nature Trail
Hoh River Trail

Hoquiam
Grays Harbor National Wildlife Refuge
  (Bowerman Basin)
Sandpiper Trail
Sewage Lagoon

Kalaloch
Ruby Beach
Six Numbered Beaches
Destruction Island
Kalaloch Lodge

Lake Quinault
South Shore Road
Rain Forest Nature Trail
Shoreline Trail
Lake Quinault Lodge
Quinault Loop Trail

La Push
First Beach
James Island
Kohchaa Island
Second Beach
Quillayute Needles
Third Beach
Mora Campground
Rialto Beach

Marrowstone Island
Fort Flagler
Marrowstone Point
Indian Island County Park
Mystery Bay State Park

Montesano
Schafer State Park
Lake Sylvia
Wynoochee Lake

Wynoochee Falls
Coho Campground
Friends Landing

Neah Bay
Makah Marina
Cape Flattery
Waatch Beach on Makah Bay
Lake Ozette
Cape Alava

North Beach
Moclips
Pacific Beach
Pacific Beach State Park
Ocean Beach Road
Roosevelt Beach
Copalis Rock
Griffiths-Priday Ocean State Park
Ocean City State Park

Ocean Shores
The ocean beach
Point Brown Jetty
Ocean Shores Golf Course
Marina
Bill's Spit
Damon Point
The Game Range
Perkins Lake
Inner Bay
Oyhut Game Habit Management Area

Port Angeles
Deer Park
City Pier
Ediz Hook
Hurricane Ridge
Heart o' the Hills Campground
Elwha River
Salt Creek Recreation Area
Salt Creek County Park
Salt Creek Estuary

Crescent Bay

Port Gamble
Harbor area
Salsbury Point County Park
Kitsap Memorial State Park

Port Orchard
Old Port Orchard Airport
Manchester State Park
Beach Drive

Port Townsend
Marina at Point Hudson
Kah Tai Lagoon (behind McDonald's)
Fort Worden
Point Wilson
Old Fort Townsend State Park
Protection Island

Poulsbo
Poulsbo Marina
Liberty Bay boardwalk
Dogfish Creek mudflats
Lemolo Drive

Quilcene
Quilcene Bay
Big & Little Quilcene estuaries
Mount Walker

Seabeck
Big Beef Creek
Seabeck Marina
Scenic Beach State Park
Guillemot Cove Nature Reserve
Wildcat Lake

Sequim
Gardiner Beach
Diamond Point
Dungeness Spit (National Wildlife Refuge)

Railroad Bridge Park (Dungeness River Audubon Center)
West Sequim Bay Park
John Wayne Marina
Marlyn Nelson County Park
Dungeness Forks
Three Crabs Road, Dungeness
Jamestown Beach

Silverdale
Clear Creek Trail
Old Mill Park

Union
Annas Bay
Lower Skokomish River

Vashon Island
Banks Road Pond
Mukai Lake
Maury Island
Point Robinson

Westport
Bottle Beach State Park
Westport Marina
Westport Jetty
Lighthouse Park
Twin Harbors State Park

131

PUBLIC GOLF COURSES

Bainbridge Island
Meadowmeer Golf & Country Club, 206/842-2218,
  golfwashington.com/courses/profiles-Meadowmeer

Bremerton
Gold Mountain Golf Complex, 360/415-5432, *goldmt.com*
Rolling Hills Golf Course, 360/479-1212, *golfwashington.com/courses/profiles-Rolling_Hills*

Elma
Oaksridge Golf Course, 360/482-3511, *golfwashington.com/courses/profiles-Oaksridge*

Gig Harbor
Madrona Links Golf Course, 253/851-5193, *madronalinks.com*

Hoodsport
Lake Cushman Golf Course, 360/877-5505, *golfwashington.com/courses/profiles-Lake_Cushman*

Ocean Shores
Ocean Shores Golf Course, 360/289-3357, *golfwashington.com/courses/profiles-Ocean_Shores*

Port Ludlow
Port Ludlow Golf Club, 800/455-0272, *portludlowresort.com*

Port Orchard
Horseshoe Lake Golf Course, 253/857-3326, *hlgolf.com*
McCormick Woods, 360/895-0130, *mccormickwoodsgolf.com*
Trophy Lake Golf & Casting, 360/874-8337, *trophylakegolf.com*
Village Greens Golf Course, 360/871-1222, *golfwashington.com/courses/profiles-Village_Greens*

Port Townsend
Chevy Chase Golf Club, 800/385-8722, *chevychasegolf.com*
Port Townsend Golf Course, 360/385-4547, *porttownsendgolf.com*

Sequim
Dungeness Golf Course, 800/447-6826, *golfdungeness.com*

Shelton
Bayshore Golf Club, 360/426-1271, *golfwashington.com/courses/profiles-Bayshore*

Union
Alderbrook Resort, 888/898-2560, *alderbrookresort.com*

PLACE NAMES

The following is the proper pronunciation of commonly mispronounced Pacific Northwest names and words. Don't embarrass yourself - take a careful look at them:

Puget Sound	PYOO-jit
Issaquah	IS-a-kwah
Mt.Rainier	ray-NEAR
Poulsbo	PAUL'S-bow (rhymes with "also")
Puyallup	pyoo-AL-up
Quilcene	QWIL-seen
Mukilteo	muckel-TEE-oh
Skagit	SKA-jit ("a" pronounced like the one in "apple")
Bothell	BAH-thul
Hoquiam	HOE-kwee-um
Moclips	MOE-clips
Kalaloch	KLAY-lock
Hoh	HOE
Montesano	mon-te-SAY-no (like "just say no")
Suquamish	SKWA-mish
Sequim	SKWIM
Willamette	wil-LAM-it (Dammit!)
Pe Ell	PEE-EL
Tenino	ten-NINE-oh
Neah Bay	NEE-uh
Roslyn	RAHZ-lin
Juan de Fuca	wahn de FYOO-kuh
Sekiu	SEE-kyoo
Anacortes	a-nuh-KOR-tus
Cle Ellum	klee-EL-um
Enumclaw	EE-num-klaw
Spokane	spoh-KAN (rhymes with "tan")
Oregon	OR-e-g'n (not "OR-e-gone")
Wenatchee	when-A-chee ("a" pronounced like the one in "apple")

Methow Valley	MET-aw
Lake Chelan	shell-AN

Oh yes, our local giant clam, the largest burrowing bivalve in the world, is the *geoduck*, pronounced "gooey-duck".

Residential Nomenclature

Now this is just for fun, but what Ron enjoys is finding out what people in a particular town or city call themselves. Europe and other parts of the US have some very poetic and romantic sounding ways of referring to the inhabitants of a community, as illustrated by the following examples:

Toronto	Torontonians
London	Londoner
Paris	Parisian
Glasgow	Glaswegian
Warsaw	Varsovian
Los Angeles	Angelino
Liverpool	Liverpudlian
Seattle	Seattleite
Rome	Roman
Aberdeen	Aberdonian
New Orleans	New Orlinian
Orkney Islands	Orkadian

The Pacific Northwest has some unusual place names, often English versions of Native American words. Unfortunately many communities never seem to have given a thought to what to call their residents. Ron has created some names based on accepted unwritten English language conventions of place-naming. In some cases, place names don't follow conventional rules of pronunciation.

He has included a column to include these anomalies.

   As a public service, Ron has either asked responsible members of those communities, or has extrapolated them following the accepted unwritten English language conventions of place-naming. If any residents take exception with the suggested form for their local labels, please contact us at rkonzak@konzak.com and we will make the correction in the next printing..

Bainbridge Island	Bainbridge Islander
Poulsbo	Poulsbovian
Suquamish	Suquamish (Native American resident)
Squamishian	(Non-Native American resident)
Indianola	Indianolan
Kingston	Kingstonian
Hansville	Hansvillian
Silverdale	Silverdallian
Bremerton	Bremertonian
Port Townsend	Port Townsender
Sequim	Sequimite
Port Angeles	Angelino
Sappho	Sapphan
Humptulips	Humptulippian
Pysht	Pyshtite
Joyce	Joycian
Sekiu	Sequin
La Push	Quileute
Seabeck	Seabecker
Brinnon	Brinnonite
Chimacum	Chimacumer
Winslow	Winslovian
Quilcene	Quilsonian
Shelton	Sheltonian
Blyn	Blynnite
Agnew	Agnuvite
Lilliwaup	Lilliwauputian
Queets	Queetser
Illahee	Illaheen
Moclips	Moclipper
Bangor	Bangorean
Hoquiam	Hoquiamite
Ilwaco	Ilwacan
Pe Ell	Pe Ellian
Port Ludlow	Luddite
Mats Mats	Mats Matser
Kalaloch	Kalalochian
Forks	You Decide!

PUBLIC INTERNET ACCESS

Use these free resources to access the web sites listed in this guide book if you are travelling without a laptop computer. The libraries will require you to register as a guest user. Check with individual library locations for directions and hours of operation.

Kitsap Regional Library *krl.org*
  Bainbridge Island, 1270 Madison N., 206/842-4162
  Downtown Bremerton, 612 5th St., 360/377-3955
  Kingston, Community Center, 11212 State Hwy 104, 360/377-3955
  Little Boston (Hansville), 31980 Little Boston Rd NE, 360/297-2670
  Port Orchard, 87 Sidney Ave, 360/876-2224
  Poulsbo, 700 NE Lincoln St, 360/779-2915
  Silverdale, 3450 NW Carlton, 360/692-2779
  Main Branch: East Bremerton, 1301 Sylvan Way, 360-405-9100,Toll-free 877/883-9900

Jefferson County Public Library, Port Hadlock *jcl.lib.wa.us*
  Port Hadlock, 620 Cedar Ave. 360/385-6544

Port Townsend Public Library *ptpl.lib.wa.us*
  Port Townsend, 1220 Lawrence Street, 360/385-3181

North Olympic Library System *nols.org*
  Port Angeles, 2210 South Peabody St, 360/417-8500
  Sequim, 630 North Sequim Ave, 360/683-1161
  Clallam Bay, Highway 112, 360/963-2414
  Forks, 171 Forks Avenue S, 360/374-6402

Timberland Regional Library *timberland.lib.wa.us*
  Hoquiam, 420 7th St, 360/532-1710
  Aberdeen, 121 East Market St, 360/533-2360
  Westport, 506 N. Montesano St, 360/268-0521
  Montesano, 125 Main Street S, 360/249-4211
  Elma, 118 N. First, 360/482-3737
  Shelton, 7th and Alder, 360/426-1362
  Hoodsport, North 40 Schoolhouse Hill Rd, 360/877-9339
  North Mason (Belfair), N.E. 23081 Highway 3, 360/275-3232

King County Library System *kcls.org/vash/home.cfm*
  Vashon Island, 17210 Vashon Hwy SW, 206/463-2069

Q

R

S

Wind Harp Press
Feedback Department

We want to hear from you! How are we doing?

What do you like about this book?

What are the areas where you would like to see improvement?

Please help us update the next printing of this book! Let us know about:

- Any errors - typos or bad information
- Dead links - web sites (they can go out of date so quickly!), phone numbers, businesses that are no longer in
- Your reviews on restaurants and lodging establishments
- New discoveries that you have made on your adventures that we need to include

You can send an email to:

feedback@windharppress.com

Or drop us a line at:

Wind Harp Press
PO Box 4494
Rolling Bay, WA 98061

Wind Harp Press
PO Box 4494
Rolling Bay, WA 98061

Order Form

For additonal copies of **Across the Sound: A Guide to Interesting Places West of Puget Sound** visit your local bookstore, order directly from our website at WindHarpPress.com or fill out the form below and mail to **Wind Harp Press, PO Box 4494, Rolling Bay, WA 98061**

Name _____

Address _____

City_____ State _____ Zip _____

Across the Sound - US $19.95 each.   Quantity _____ Extended Price _____

Washington State residents please add $1.72 per book.   _____
Allow 4-6 weeks for delivery.

Shipping and Handling Options
❑ US Mail Book Rate $3.00 for the first book.   Shipping & Handling _____
 $2.00 for each additional book
❑ US Mail by Air $5.00 for the first book,
 $3.00 for each additional book.
❑ Outside US, $9.00 for the first book,
 $5.00 for each additional book   Total Enclosed   _____

Please make all payments in US funds to **Wind Harp Press**
Payment: ❑ Check   ❑ Money Order ❑ Credit Card

Card number _____ Expiration Date _____

Name on Card _____ Signature _____